SEO
for
Startups

(Aman Tandon)

SEO for Startups
Copyright © Aman Tandon, 2018
First published in the Year 2018 by Gamahouse Publishing
(www.gamahouse.com)

Edited and typeset by Edioak (www.edioak.com)

Devoted to the spirit of learning and being
grateful every moment.

Table of Contents

About the Author

Aman is a professor of digital marketing at Chandigarh University, and he writes books, which considering where you are reading this makes perfect sense. He is best known for having being worked as a hacker, columnist, making the central database of hospitals in India that do organ donation and for gamification of learning initiatives.

Aman has spent the last decade reading, learning, experimenting with digital marketing projects ranging from colleges, startups, bloggers, lawyers, hospitals, charted accountants, real estate, doctors and politicians.

He loves teaching, writing, and his Love involves around making Marketing Strategies for Brands.

Blog – *www.amantandon.com*

1. Introduction

SEO stands for Search Engine Optimization. It is a process of increasing the visibility of a website for "free" on organic or natural results. You search something on Google or Yahoo or any search engine, and in turn, it gives a long list of magical pages. Understanding the algorithm that ranks these pages is SEO.

It is all about ranking on the first page of the search engine. Have you ever clicked on the 2nd page or 3rd for a result? We prefer first page and top 3 listings. This book is about how to rank on the top.

 Let us say you have a bakery in Chandigarh and you rank for keywords like "Best Bakery in Chandigarh," "Bakery near me," "Home Cooked Bakery in Chandigarh" so the quantity and quality of the traffic will increase on your website which will lead to more sales.

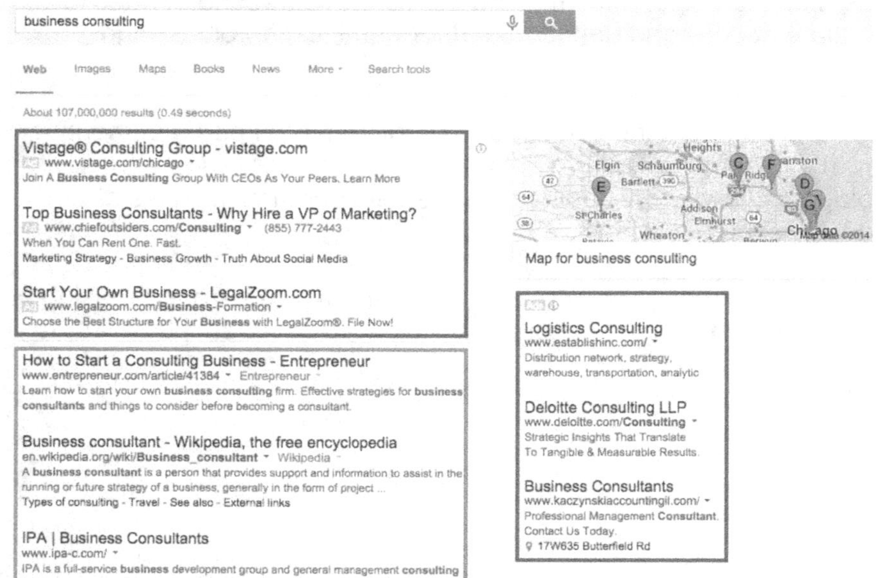

As you can see in the above image, we have organic and paid results. Organic results are ranked based on your merit, and these results are natural, whereas, for paid, you have to pay based on the competition, like in Covid19 Advertisement Rate for all the Networks like Facebook and Google have increased.

Ranking organic is vital as more than 81% of the traffic is from search engines.

This book is all about how you can rank organic in search results without paying loads of money to search engines.

So, let's get started.

To your success and ranking.

Aman Tandon

2. SEO Basics

This chapter may look like the second one in the book, but this one was last to get written as defining the basics of SEO that are not covered in the subsequent chapters was gritty. So, if it looks like a short chapter, thank the publisher and get ready for a roller coaster ride ahead.

These basics will lay your foundation for a multistorey building. So, unless you have built a ground floor, do not start the construction of subsequent levels. Let us get underway: -

1.Title Tag

The title tag should be 55-60 characters long as more than that will not show on the search engines.

IMS Noida - Top Ranked MBA Management Colleges In Delhi NCR ...
www.imsnoida.in/ ▾
IMS **Noida** is one of the top management colleges in Delhi NCR. It provides advanced knowledge of the field to the students and is ranked as one of the top MBA ...
You've visited this page 3 times. Last visit: 5/7/16

→ Pipes

Top 10 Colleges in NOIDA | Best Ten Colleges in NOIDA NCR Delhi
www.delhieducation.net/**colleges/top**-10-**colleges-in-noida**-ncr-delhi.aspx ▾
Feb 13, 2013 - Higher Education in NOIDA, NCR Delhi: Another reason of interest in industrial town NOIDA. Colleges in NOIDA, National Capital Region ...

The first link has title length of more than 60 words, and as we exceed the three dots gets displayed instead of our full title. The second link can be an example of an optimized title based on characters.

In the second link "Top 10 colleges in NOIDA" and" BEST Ten Colleges in NOIDA NCR Delhi" are separated by pipes |.

Use the following to separate keywords in your title tag:
1. Pipes |
2. Comma ,

If your company name is prime like in the image above" IMS Noida" is the name and since people will be searching this term a lot so it is placed in front but if your company name is not relevant than adding it after the title like *My title – Company or My title | Company.*You can even remove it as we see in the second link above.

Never stuff title tags to rank like let's say you are selling doors made of Plastic, Wood & Iron.

Keyword stuffed title – *Iron Doors | Plastic Doors | Wood Doors | All Types of Doors | Plastic Doors and More| Mydoor.com*

Optimized Title – *Iron, Plastic and Wood Doors | Doors | Mydoor.com*

 Use action words in your title tag like Get, Take, Boost, Learn, and Go. To make your headlines stand out use "Portent Title Generator" and "Sumo Title Generator"

2. Meta Description

The meta description is defined as it is a snippet which consists of a maximum 155 characters and it is a tag sort in an HTML. It is also responsible for summarizing the whole content available on the page. As the name suggests that it is a proper description of what is being said and available on the web page.

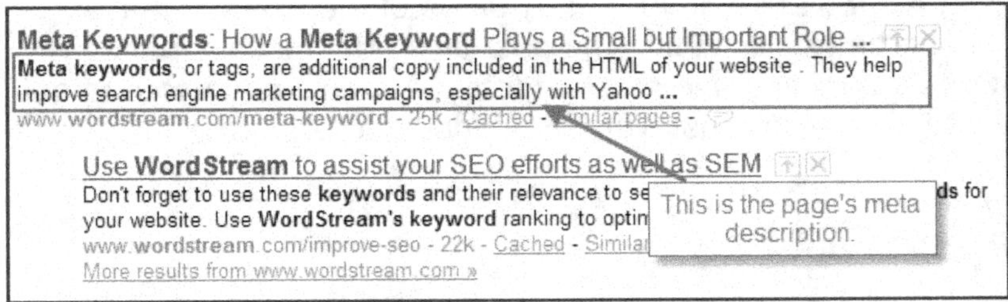

3.Internal Linking

Internal linking as the name sounds is linking internally within a domain. Let's say, for example, content A is linking out to content B and content C on the same website.

When you start internal linking, you rank better for keywords. *Code:<a href=http://yourdomain.com/"> Visit our Marketing Tutorial </a>*

Instead of "yourdomain", you can put the URL of the post and instead of 'Visit our Marketing Tutorial' you can type the keyword that you want to rank for. Don't overdo this.

Generally, the maximum number of posts that you should link to in a single post is five to remain interactive with the user. Avoid hyperlinks that say *click here or a link to the homepage or the contact page.*

Internal Linking gives you the following benefits –

- If the user likes what you have written, then he gets a chance to read more of your posts.
- Google will crawl your site faster when you use internal linking for at least four months.
- It will improve your ranking for paramount keywords and even related keywords that you might not be even aware of.

At every point in time that you want to write a new post, think about a post you have made earlier on that has similarities to the present one you are writing. At any stage of the write up that you know it can be referenced to the past post add the links naturally to your new post and use an anchor text that relates to your target keyword for an older post, you are trying to link.

4. URL Structure

A friendly URL means an address that could define the post. This is how you can rank multiple places of a business through friendly URLs

www.mybusiness.com/places/newyork
www.mybusiness.com/places/newdelhi

URLs should be filled with keywords that you want to target. See how Lynda.com targeted training in their URL. Their post name is Audio+Music tutorials.

Another thing to remember is the structure of the URLs.

To write an optimized post, we use post name, but you can use custom structure if you are targeting some specific keywords. Above customizations are offered by most of the blogging platforms.

Avoid using prepositions and Articles like a, an, for, and to. Short URLs are easy to share over Email, Whatsapp, and over thousands of digital products.

5. Mobile Friendly

Sites should have less data in terms of design, offering or any features than full content, which means writings ought to be cut into brief and concise variants. Web designers and marketing specialists additionally face a new test of improving highlights, duplicates, and word check without expelling first choices.

The basic methodology of web designers is to make the structure responsive but when the site is responsive it means that whole content will be shown. So it is a very good idea that you have a huge website with plenty of pages , consider making a different mobile website.

6. Crawl Accessibility

If the search engine is unable to crawl your site, there is no chance your post is going to get ranked in the search engine. Crawling implies the ability of the search engine's bot/crawler/spider to scan a website for necessary information like titles, images, keywords, and other linked pages.

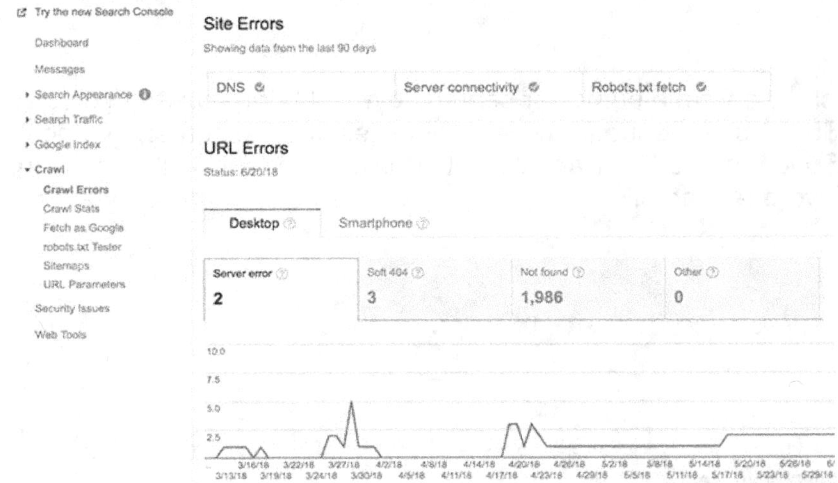

Check for all the errors from Google Webmaster Console.

3. Keyword Research

Each sale from a particular search keyword brings on an average of $5000 as revenue for college websites, it brings on an average of 500 to $1000 for any website design firm. This is the magic of keyword research.

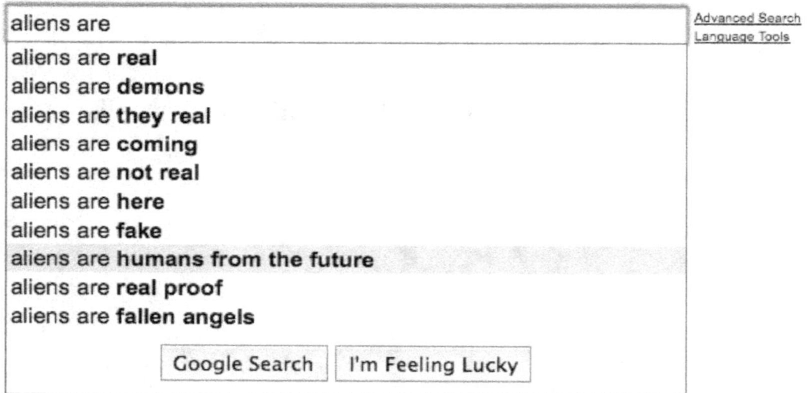

What are keywords? Keywords are words or phrases curious searchers insert on the search bar of search engines in an attempt to directly land on the ideal page that will answer their questions.

Since almost all businesses have found themselves spaces online, everyone wants to be the first to pop up when keywords relating to their services/niches are queried on the search engines. For this reason, over time, the needs for the utilization of **top quality keywords has grown to a significant level.**

Not every website gets the same result on the search engine. Some are more popular than others, and as a result, they rank much higher. The difference between the popular ones and those that are not popular is the effect of the keywords they utilize and other ranking factors like Backlinks, Site Speed, On page and off page optimization and so on.

Keyword research means identification of the ideal words or phrases that a website needs to contain so that it can be ranked on the first page in the major search engines like Google, Bing, Yahoo, etc. For a website to stand a chance of being ranked in major search engines, the first task is to delve into quality keyword research.

Reliable and working keyword research can throw your business on the first page on search engines. Keyword research is an "everybody wins the game". Curious customers get to find what they are looking for without much stress while service providers/product sellers get to connect with their potential customers.

In short, answer this question. What should your customers search so that they find your business?

Low Competition and High Competition

Any website owner who gives little or no attention to use keyword research will end up using the wrong keywords that won't take the site any far. In the process of carrying out keyword research, it is imperative to recognize keyword competition (keyword difficulty) factor. Keyword competition is split into two: **low competition keyword** and **high competition keyword.**

Low competition keywords are those keywords that are not common with many websites. That is, they are not over-used by other competitors. High competition keywords are the keywords a vast number of sites have incorporated in their contents. Utilizing this type of keywords can delay your website more than necessary before it gets ranked.

Low competition keywords are far better because it's not yet saturated and has less keyword difficulty. *Keyword difficulty* is a strong factor you need to observe when researching ideal keywords.

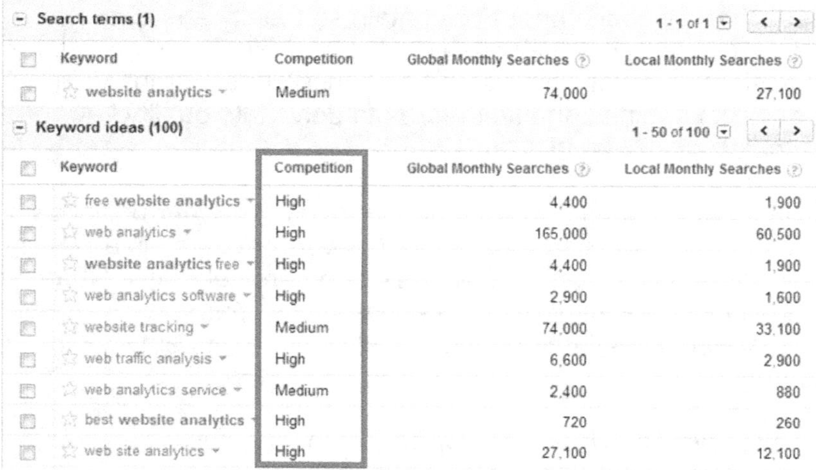

The higher the value of keyword difficulty, the tighter it is to compete with sites using similar keywords. Giving attention to low competition keyword can quicken the SEO success of a website.

How Do You Know Your Keyword is a Longtail or Short Tail?

Long tail keywords are not familiar with other competitors because they are specific to your service or niche. These keywords used to contain 3-4 words. It can help your customers to locate your store on the internet directly. Example of long tail keywords is "make money at home", "straighten your rough hair."

Short tail keywords contain one word or a maximum of two. They are not specific because of their lengths; as such, they cannot narrow customers' searches to what they are truly expecting to see. Examples are "rough hair", "money", "dirty car", etc.

3.1 Who needs Keyword Research?

This is the era businesses and service providers have been able to increase their earnings and productivities twice, three times (even more) more than ever before. Leveraging the benefit of a vast number of people coming on the internet every day to get answers to their questions has offered them the excellent opportunity to connect with their customers and finally make sales.

Two categories of people who need keyword research are:
- Service providers
- Product sellers

Service providers are the individuals or companies who operate to make money but have nothing to do with sales of goods.

Examples of service providers are:
- Accountant/Accounting firm
- Lawyer/ Law firm
- Engineer
- Web developer
- Software Developer
- Writer/Writing firm, etc.

Product sellers are individual or companies that derive their revenues from the sales of products. If they have websites, they can utilize the benefits of keyword research and enhance their presence right in front of their potential buyers on the internet.

In a nutshell, anyone with an online presence needs Keyword Research.

3.2 Ways & Tools

1. **Brainstorm** – Brainstorm and jot down every keyword that you think your customer might search on an Excel sheet. For this exercise, make sure all your internal stakeholders are present. Also, list down all the features and advantages of the product to come with better ideas during brainstorming sessions.

2. **Talk to your customers**- This will give you exact phrases of what they think and search about your product. Let's say you have built an Inverter that has advanced functionalities like 19 Hours Backup, Gold Plated Inside, Diamond Plated outside, 1Kg weight and available for a dollar. Well, instead of doing SEO for the above terms, ask them. You might get suggestions like "Cheap Inverter" or "Highest Backup Inverter". This reduces much effort since USP for us might not be a searchable query for the user.

    Email, call or get a questionnaire filled by the customer of what he thinks about the product.

3. **Google and Youtube Advanced Search Suggestions**

The suggestions that you see above are what other people are searching. So it is an excellent idea to research via advanced search. However, manually typing every letter to get suggestion can be very tiresome so use Ubersuggest or keywordtool.io

Alternatives suggestions of search engine can also be tried like of Yahoo, Bing DuckDuckGo Ecosia and Dogpile.

4.   Google Trends

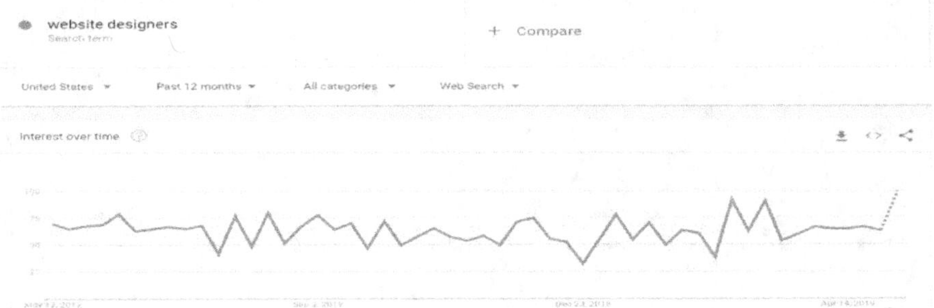

 Google Trend shows you a graph of how a particular keyword is performing over a period of time. This can give you an idea, whether or not your keyword is still searched over the Internet. You can download the data as well.

5.   Ubersuggest

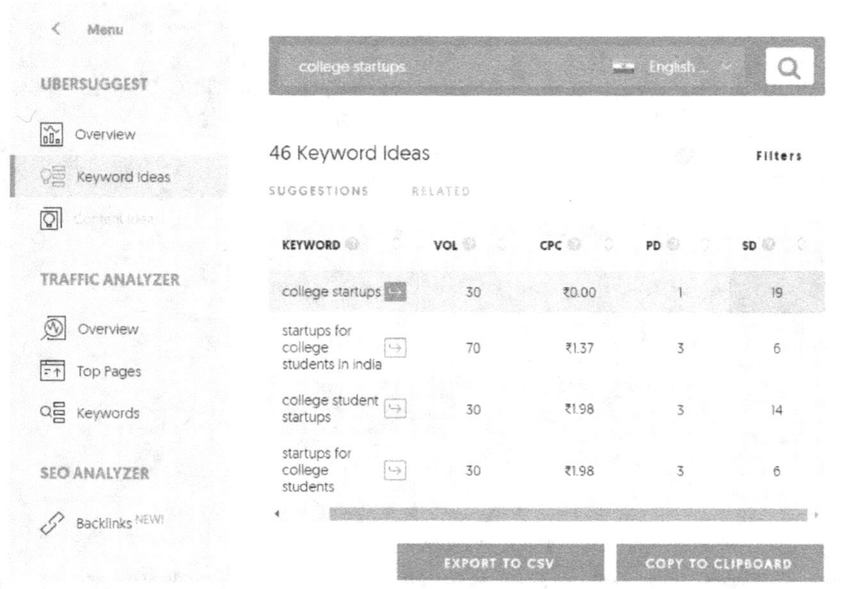

With this excellent free tool, you can get fresh and unique long tail keywords. Apart from the keyword ideas, you can also see the top pages that are ranking for that keyword with backlinks analyzer as well.

6. Wordtracker

Wordtracker is also a free keyword suggestion tool, but it gives related keyword suggestions for a particular keyword.

Lets says if I am searching for "College Startups". Related Keywords that people search would be Investing, Business Ideas or Network as you can see in the blog post above. This helps us in making a comprehensive guide on any subject which includes all the related terms.

7. Keywordtool.io

Keywordtool.io is a paid tool that is most advanced amongst the above since it contains combined functionalities of all the tools.

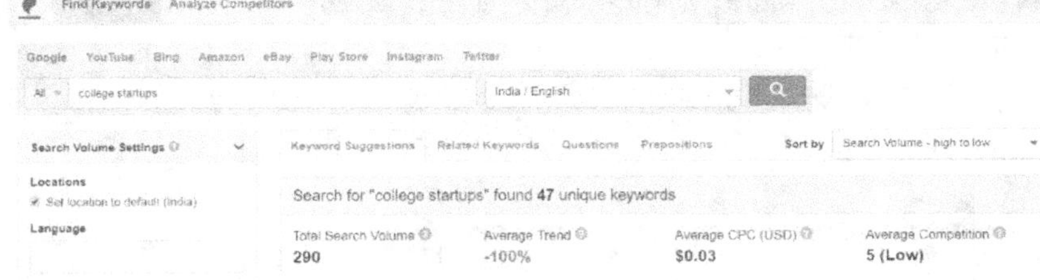

A. You can analyze competition in-depth from this tool.

B. You can switch from Google suggestions to, YouTube, Bing, Amazon, eBay, Playstore, Instagram and Twitter Suggestions. So it is a suggestions tool that contains almost data from everything.

C. You can find a related keyword for a particular keyword. Know that if you search Cat Family, you might see pictures of Leopard. Google understands the related keyword.

Conclusion

Keyword research is essential, but the focus should be on quality content. High-Quality content without keyword research can make you reach your destination via staircase if you live on the 48th floor of a building, but proper keyword research for a blog post is like taking a lift to the 48th floor of a building.

4. Site Architecture

Imagine you visit a library with thousands of books. You need to access book in the science section of an author whose name starts with J. Well in some scenarios this segmentation would be easy as sorting has been done but imagine all the books are kept together without any segmentation or order. This would take months to sort the book. This is how search engine bots are even confused when the architecture of the website is not defined. It merely refers to telling what is where and how page and post orders are defined.

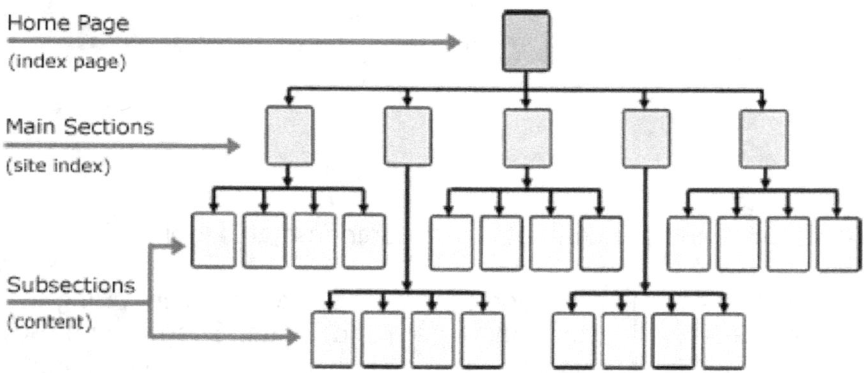

Website architecture is the way we structure a website to ensure that we achieve our business goals while providing an excellent experience for our users.

Site architecture is drawn to leave a lasting impression on your visitors; you need to create experiences that go beyond those of a simple and usable website. It merely plays a different role in web design and is now the basis of excellent user experience. Usability means user-centered design. The design and development process is focused on the potential user - to ensure that their goals, mental models, and requirements are met - to design effective and easy-to-use products.

A high-quality user interface is vital in the sense that it is easier for your target audience to see clearly what your products are. It is designed to display the services you offer unambiguously, to attract the attention of your visitors and keep them on your site. In simple terms, a good user interface is essential because it can turn potential visitors into buyers because it facilitates interactions between the user and your website or web application. When you scratch under the surface, you realize that the user interface is a reasonably complex domain that involves anticipating the user's preferences and then creating an interface that understands and respects those preferences. The user interface focuses not only on aesthetics but also maximizes the responsiveness, efficiency, and accessibility of a website.

Everything is not about the design architecture of a website. It is about content. It is not enough for your website to be precise; your content must also be relevant. It is necessary for you to know your users and why they visit your site.

1. Start by defining who your users are.

2. Second, talk to them about what their goals are when visiting your site.

3. Third, define the user scenarios that show, in which situation visitors are visiting your site and what are the goals that you would want them to complete.

Any design decision you make should result in a more user-friendly website for your users.

For Example; Apple has done an excellent job in giving priority to its content by focusing on its users.

The brand offers smartphones and other accessories related to technology. When you visit their website, you can choose to browse their store by Mac, iPhone or Watch, or Apple TV which leads to faster results as compared to grouping on the basis of age , location , choice or previous browsing history of the user.

4.1 Making a Site Architecture

1.Make an Association Plan

The first step is to sit down and find the best way to organize your website. If you have a small site of fewer than ten pages, this part should be quite simple (although it is still essential to do it!). If you have a more prominent website with tens or hundreds of pages, it will be a bit more complicated.

Try to keep the hierarchy of your site as simple and straightforward as possible. Unless you have an unusually large site containing thousands of pages, your link structure should not be more than three levels deep. Ideally, a user should never be more than three clicks away from another page of the website.

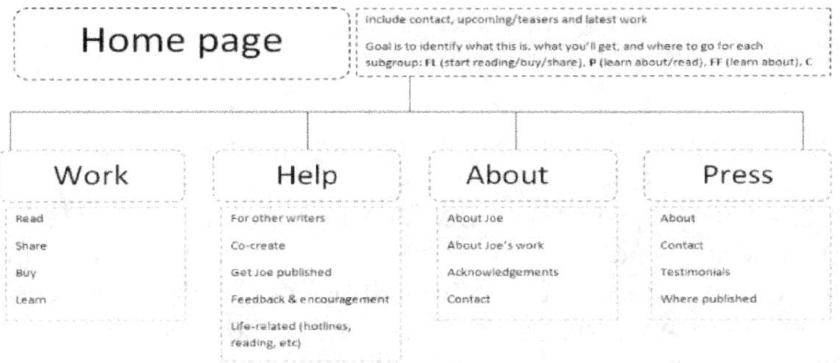

In the above example, the perfect demonstration of the alignment of toolbars and the topics is set according to the ease of the viewers. The user who comes to this website doesn't have a hard time finding the content of this site because he can see all the things in the toolbar of this website. The user can view almost every page of the website in just 2-3 clicks. This shows that less click game is more important to make site architecture attractive and user-friendly.

2.Characterize your Primary Categories

Think about the main categories in which you can divide your pages:

- Description of what are the different pages and products
- How does a visitor browse a particular group?

Do not choose your categories arbitrarily; they must be based on useful information for your end user. Think first about how they search and browse, then structure your website based on that.

For example, for an online bookstore, it may be possible to divide your products into categories such as the length, author, number of words as Amazon Kindle does it but most site visitors will find it more comfortable to see your products divided into categories such as fiction, nonfiction, and common genres.

3. The Priority of the Content

Websites for a Smartphone with different screen resolutions is the biggest challenge in the world. While desktop sites often contain a wide range of content, mobile sites usually include only the most crucial functions as time essential and you can populate everything on a Mobile site as the loading time will be high.

Desktop Site:

Mobile Site:

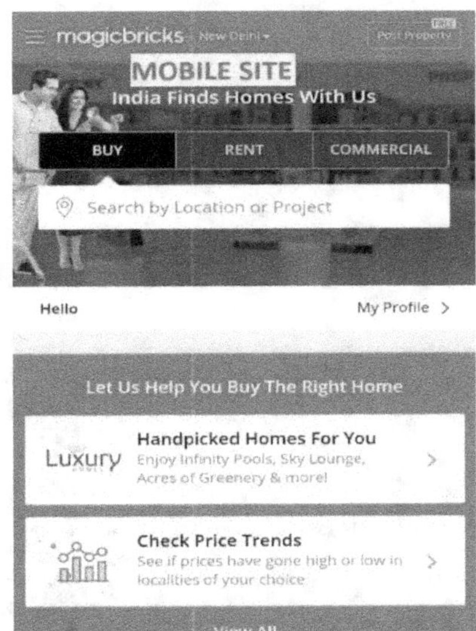

Mobile site designs should give priority to the site, and the users are more likely to use a mobile device. Having insights into your customers' needs dictates a lot from a content-development standpoint, and a site's architecture and screen layouts.

4. Menus

On the desktop, it is common to have mega-menus with many categories and subcategories. This type of configuration is ideal for desktop users who have screens large enough to read the text in these menus and easily click text links. It's different on the mobile, of course, because the screens are small. Mobile menus should be designed with these elements in mind. This means having a single-level menu as we can see in the example.

Desktop Site

Mobile Site

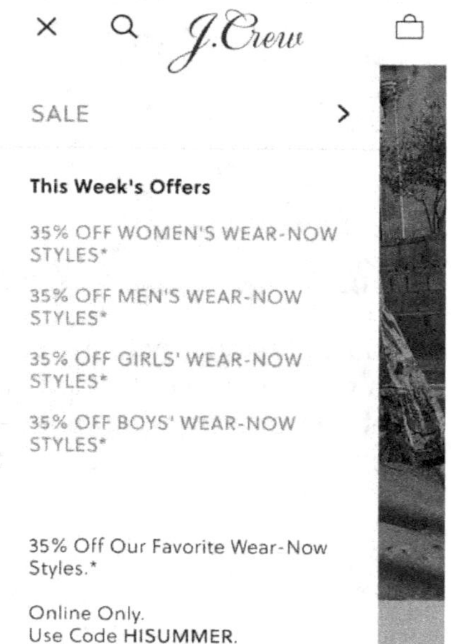

Conclusion

Effective *Site Architecture* enables a great user and search engine experience. While we are designing site architecture we should not let user think about what is where in our website and also keeping in mind that everything is under 3 clicks of a mouse button.

5. Google Ranking

Google algorithm is a complex system used to retrieve data and instantly deliver the best possible results for a query. It uses a combination of algorithms and many ranking signals to provide web pages ranked by relevance on its search engine result pages.

S. N	Year	Number of Updates
1	2009	400
2	2010	516
3	2011	538
4	2012	665
5	2013	890
6	2016	1653
7	2017	2453
8	2018	3234

A website that Google ranks on the first page is reviewed for more than 200 factors. If a website managed to be on the first page, it does not necessarily mean that it will last here for tomorrow as well, Google reviews and updates its algorithm for more times than we could imagine.

Why Google needs an Algorithm?

Initially, Google used to rollout very few changes to its algorithm, but now thousands are rolling out every year. Google uses different algorithms to check the quality of the content. Before the appearance of search engines like Google, Yahoo, and Bing, one of the ways made for discovering data was through web directories.

 However, over time, there were many websites which didn't provide relevant detail as per the needs of the user, but still, they were able to rank using Black Hat Techniques of Link Building , Cloaking, Spinning Articles and just ranking needed some serious attention from Google's Point of view.

These websites which had a high bounce rate and low average session duration time, which meant the user was not satisfied with the webpage quality.

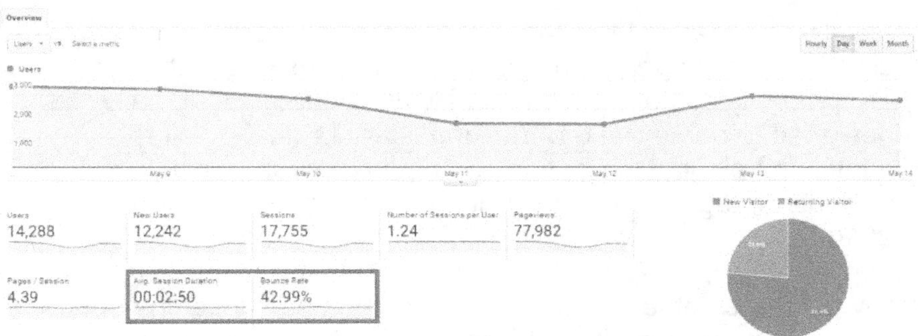

That's where the need for algorithm rose. Now the algorithm checks the details of the websites, its downtime, content, backlinks, shares, how much time a person spent on the site, and many such factors.

Naturally, no magic tricks are going to work for you in case of google ranking. However, by paying attention to the factors mentioned below and throughout the book, you can be sure to boost your rankings.

5.1 Major Updates by Google

GOOGLE ALGORITHM	PANDA	PENGUIN	HUMMINGBIRD
SEARCH	CONTENT	BACK-LINKS	ANSWERS, NOT KEYWORDS
WIN	Well-written content Informative content Low bounce rate	Natural back-links Natural anchor text profile	Longer content Wider range of words Content written to deliver direct answers
LOSE	Thin content Duplicate content Auto-generate content Content farm	Over optimised content Keywords stuffing Low quality back-links Links schemes	Thin content keyword based Keyword based optimisation

Panda Algorithm Update

Initially released in February 2011, Google's Panda algorithm creates a webpage "score" based on a series of quality criteria that are primarily content-driven and always updated. Originally designed to behave like a "ranking filter" for filtering sites containing plagiarized or thin content from search results, Panda was later integrated into the primary ranking algorithm in early 2016.

Try to create content that responds to the user's search queries without ever copying it. Get Panda's attention with long-form content that's up to ten times that of the competition.

Penguin Algorithm Update

Google began the Penguin update in April 2012 to all the websites that did blackhat link building methods like purchasing links or getting them through connection networks of low-quality websites planned principally to increase Google rankings. At the point when another Penguin update was discharged, sites that have made a move to expel awful links were considered for ranking again.

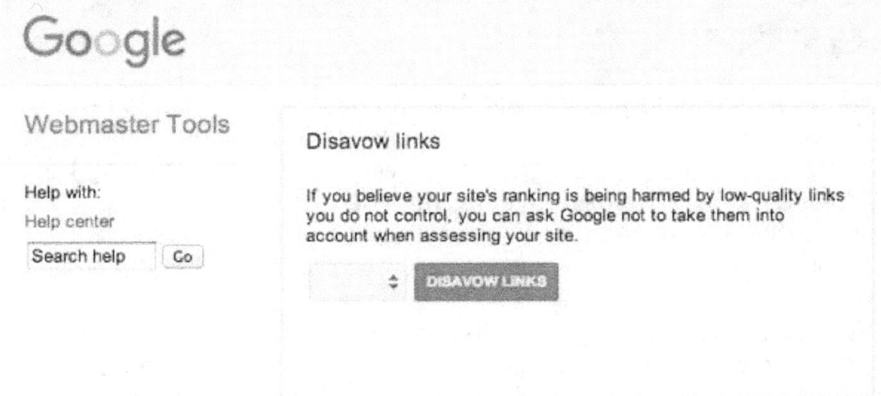

You can use the Google Disavow tool (https://www.google.com/webmasters/tools/disavow-links) to remove low-quality backlinks.

Hummingbird Algorithm Update

In the fall of 2013, Google rolled out yet another algorithm update. Google Humminbird focuses on answers, not keywords in a blog post. It sees whether a query satisfies the user's intent to its fullest. It overrides and ranks content which answers user queries directly.

Google is focusing on the complete form of content. It means a single blog post which serves as a guide and has all the subtopics in a field that any user searches. See Subchapter named "Complete Content" in Advanced Blog Optimization.

5.2 Factors affecting your Google Ranking

Age of Domain

Google considers any website less than six months old to be a "new" site. This means how long the website has been online and active, not how long someone has owned the corresponding URL. You've had a URL for ten years, but you only created and posted a live website last week then, according to the Google search engine, your site is only a week old.

So, it also depends on how often do you update your blog posts. But purchasing old domains that were active and have a good domain authority could rank you quicker. This is a paradox.

Older sites are considered more reliable and less likely to post false or unverified information. However, Sites less than six months old increase search rankings slowly.

Purchase domains for five years. This shows search engines that your business website is here to stay for a long period.

Content quality

Google's robot works continuously to ensure that the content of a website is as fresh and relevant as possible for users.
Google takes into account several elements like

1. Length of Content

According to experts, the top 10 ranked pages contains more than 2000 words. Usually, the longer a website's content, the more credible a site will be concerning the search index. Posts must always be at least 300 words long to ensure a good ranking. However, longer posts, consisting of 1,000 to 3,000 words, are even more powerful. A more detailed content tells Google that your website is an actual authority on the subject it covers.

2. Post Timeliness

Another thing that Google takes into account is the frequency with which you post new content on your website. Spider bots have a big appetite and will not be happy with old and outdated content that stays idle on your site for weeks, months, and years at a time without any interaction with the users. It is your job to keep these bots well fed. And you can do that by producing a steady stream of fresh content for them to feast on.

If you publish new content at least two or three times a week, the content of your website will be analyzed, indexed, and added to Google's search index much more quickly.

3. Original Content

Google's crawlers can index an entire website in seconds while simultaneously referencing all of its content to all other sites in the search index. Do not try to pull one fast and throw mountains of plagiarized or duplicated content on your website. Even if you rank for a shorter period of time you will be penalized.

#1   75% similar

"How To Use The Screaming Frog For those of you that like to keep an eye on your backlinks and check to see if they are still where they should be, it can be a laborious task"

https://www.screamingfrog.co.uk/how-to-use-the-screaming-frog-seo-spider-tool-to-audit-backlinks-2/

...Backlinks ScreamingGraeme Posted 22 September, 2011 by ScreamingGraeme in Screaming Frog SEO Spider How To Use The Screaming Frog SEO Spider Tool To Audit Backlinks email facebook twitter For those of you that like to keep an eye on your backlinks and check to see if they are still where they should be, it can be a laborious task. Perhaps you have a list of links from sources which need to be checked that they are still in place...

Check if a content is plagirised from a premium service like www.quetext.com or a free service like www.duplichecker.com

Quality Backlinks

Links to your website from legitimate, verified high-quality sources improve your ranking in the Google search index. The best way to get this type of quality backlinks is to publish excellent, useful, and relevant content. The kind of material that real people will want to use and share with others.

Clean Domain Affects

Having a "clean domain" means if your website has even been marked for trying to deceive the search index system.
To do this, penalized sites use too many keywords ("Keyword Stuffing") or buy fraudulent "backlinks" (links to your websites from spammed and poorly rated content sites). Keep up with the organic backlinks of the highest quality.

Chapters in the Book

Most of the chapters in this book like Local SEO , Site Architecture and Link Building to name a few directly affect your rankings. So consider them too as ranking factors.

6. Local SEO

Local SEO is about increasing visibility of Businesses that serve the communities physically. It is a process of making your business be visible in local search results.

Businesses that have a particular location and serve the customers in a specific geographical area can boost walkins and sales revenue.

It includes everything from claiming the listing , managing rating and reviews and popularity so that you rank on top.

For Example:

Doctors near me
Lawyers in [City Name]

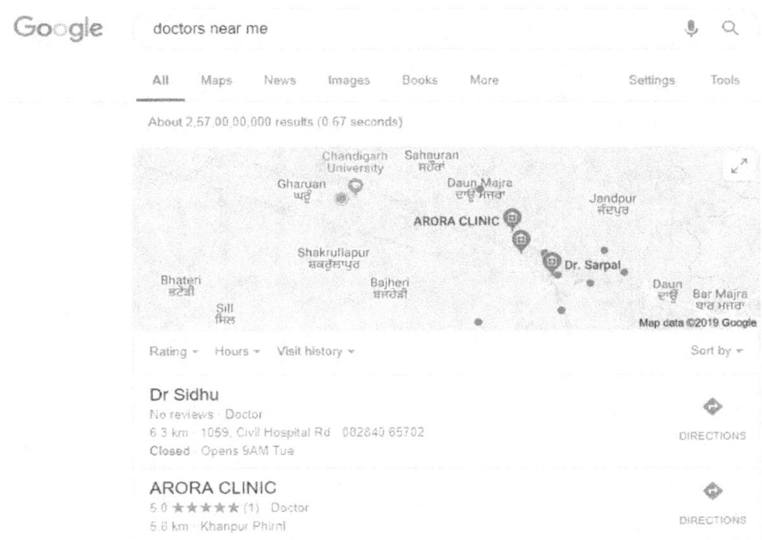

The reason every business owner should focus on Local SEO is that more than 46% of the Search Intent for Google's Algorithm is Local. Nearby shops, companies, colleges appear in the search result for the same queries even when big corporations with lots of reviews are already present.

6.1 Importance of Local SEO

52% of the people who did a local search on their phone went to physical store within two days, and 34% of the desktop users did the same. People are fascinated when they know something is nearby, and their solutions can be quick.

Following are the most prominent reasons for people taking decisions:-

Local Options Online

In this age of Internet being at home, people can search for the information they want. If an individual wants to buy an Air conditioner, he does an online search to find the best options available locally. Google My Business shows up with the nearest AC shops that help the customer to visit the nearest outlet.

Maximum Conversion Rate

56% of the people who search for local businesses take action within a day or immediately make a purchase. This happens because people searching for Local Business are in urgent need to purchase something. Plus, searching for a local business attracts the customer to visit the place just because they are in need and the shop is nearest to the customer.

Let's suppose I come back home after a hard day and craving for the pizza. I will search online for the nearest pizza shop, select the best pizza, and do order there. Because I want the delivery to be quick, I don't want to wait an hour even if it is quality. The convenience of the customer concerning location and time is how the local SEO increases your conversion rate.

Quality Reviews = Sales

Your website is the online brand of your business. With the help of local SEO, you enable your users to interact more easily with your business. You can ask users to give their reviews about your

services. People prefer to consult the opinions of other customers before buying anything.
While purchasing anything and taking a decision online, people see what the average rating of the product or services that they are ordering.

Customer Reviews

⭐⭐⭐☆☆ 11,201

2.8 out of 5 stars ▾

5 star		44%
4 star		9%
3 star		6%
2 star		7%
1 star		34%

Share your thoughts with other customers

Write a customer review

Will you order the product above which has three star ratings? That is how perception regarding reviews is built.

6.2 Ranking Factors

There are more than thousand ranking factors, and if we combined them, it would be a 6 part book series. My publisher, me and you reading certainly don't want it right? So here are the most critical factors that affect your Google My Business ranking.

Google My Business Page

Chandigarh University

| Website | Directions | Save |

Private university in Ajitgarh, Punjab · 550.0 m

Chandigarh University is a private university located on NH-95, Chandigarh-Ludhiana Highway, Mohali, Punjab, India. Wikipedia

Address: NH-95, Ludhiana - Chandigarh State Hwy, Punjab 140413

Vice-Chancellor: Dr. R.S. Bawa

Chancellor: Satnam Singh Sandhu

Google My Business is the most critical part of local SEO. Many people find your business online because of Google My Business listings and decide if they want to become a customer. The initial phase is to claim your Google My Business. You want to claim

ownership of your My Business listing so you can include all the information that potential customers need.
Link to claim your listing:
https://www.google.com/intl/en_in/business/

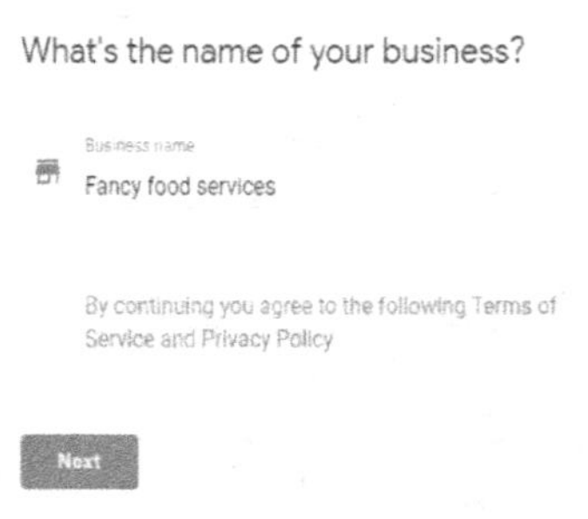

Here is the list of all the information which is necessary to make your Google My Business page catchy and attractive:
- Company name, address and telephone number
- Link to their official website
- Working hours and holidays
- Their category of business
- Google Map pin on their location
- Photos and videos of 30 seconds of your business (This can lead to faster and quality conversions)
- Links to specific actions such as online orders or bookings

Google My Business Posts

Google My Business posts is a great chance to post your events, offers, posts, updates, or anything that you would like your customers to know. Posting events and offers gets you indexed and ranking very quickly.

Wired Production Group ⭐

Event management company in Cedar
Rapids, Iowa · 1.7 mi

Website   Directions

Address: 2037 N Towne Ln NE, Cedar Rapids, IA 52402

Hours: Open today · 8AM–5PM ▾

Phone: (319) 294-9410

Suggest an edit

Wired Production Group
on Google

Posts on Google My Business receives the highest engagement of all the ways mentioned in the ranking factors.

Google My Business Category

Google My Business category communicates about a company or which division of business it belongs to. The division is also relevant if you are trying to rank keywords in the Google search engine. Choosing the right categories can positively affect your ranking in Google Maps.

Ensure that the main category you use for your business is the best choice, based on the products, services, or goals of your business.

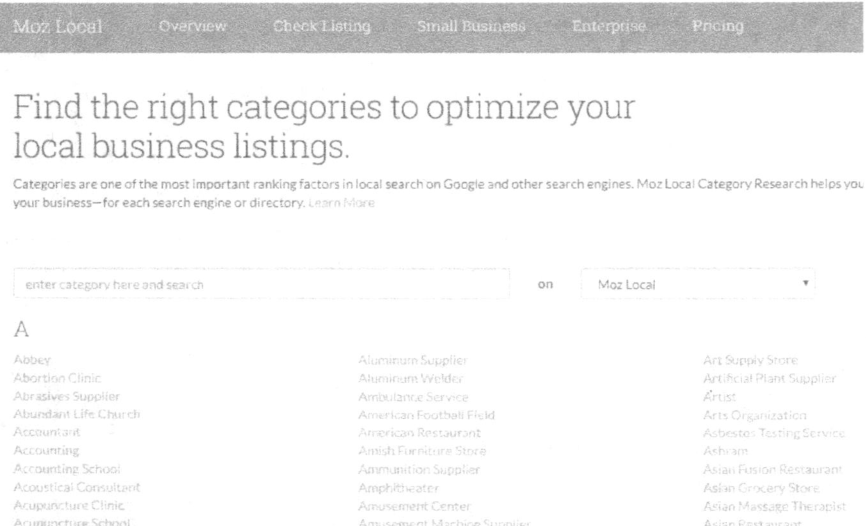

Moz has prepared a massive list of categories that your business might belong to:

Check them out here: https://moz.com/local/categories

Photos

Businesses with photos receive a higher number of requests for directions and clicks on their websites than those who have not yet uploaded the pictures. People perceive this as that the business is running and this is the reason the photos are uploaded. This translates to more customers for you, which translates into more profit for you.

In the above example, we have photos of a college named IMS Noida, which posted pictures about farewell, libraries, classrooms, playgrounds, and the overall infrastructure and environment through photos. Which indeed results in quality clicks to their listings.

It is important to have photos on your list, but you cannot stop there. If you want to compete with other companies, you need to make sure you add the right photos, optimize them, and update them regularly. By doing so, you stay in the top companies list in Google's search results.

The photos in Google My Business list are significant to customers as they get attracted. It's a reason for them to choose you or your competitors. Photos are the first thing people notice that differentiates your company from all the other companies in the search results. These may include inside or outside shots of your store or office front, team photos, logos, or images of your products or services in action.

Bing Places for Business

Just like Google my Business, Bing has Bing Places for Business. Bing has much less competition and a more conversational user base in many places, making it perfect for small, specific campaigns targeting specific customer groups. Some argue that Bing could also have a lower bounce rate than Google, which means visitors could view more pages and click more links. Bing has fewer Google algorithm rigidity, so less hard work is required to rank.

Claim your Bing Listing from www.bingplaces.com

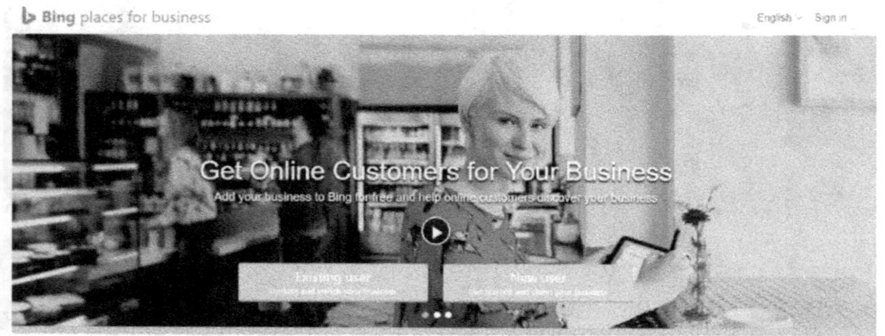

Add your business to Bing in 3 easy steps

In summary, Bing's Places for Business can be worth it, especially if you have an old site in a particular area. It won't surpass Google at any point shortly, which is not a shock, but as part of a broader strategy, it has its small place.

Online Local Directories

Directories are a great way to get backlinks to a company's website. Since Google considers many of these "quote" sites to be reliable and quality websites, the list of a local business listed in a directory can often be included in early search engine results, which is a huge bonus. In fact, many of these high-quality online business directories dominate the first search results. Moreover, there are thousands of online directories and sometimes specific to a particular location which you should mainly focus on for Local SEO.

Example of online directories in India are Justdial, Sulekha, and Grotal.

Number of Positive Reviews

Encourage satisfied customers to post reviews online. This does not mean that you should ask for reviews or purchase them. Let the reviews be genuine. Because when you do so, the chances are that you will rank below sites that have lesser reviews than you. Google Algorithm does not focus on the number of reviews; it focuses on the quality of reviews.

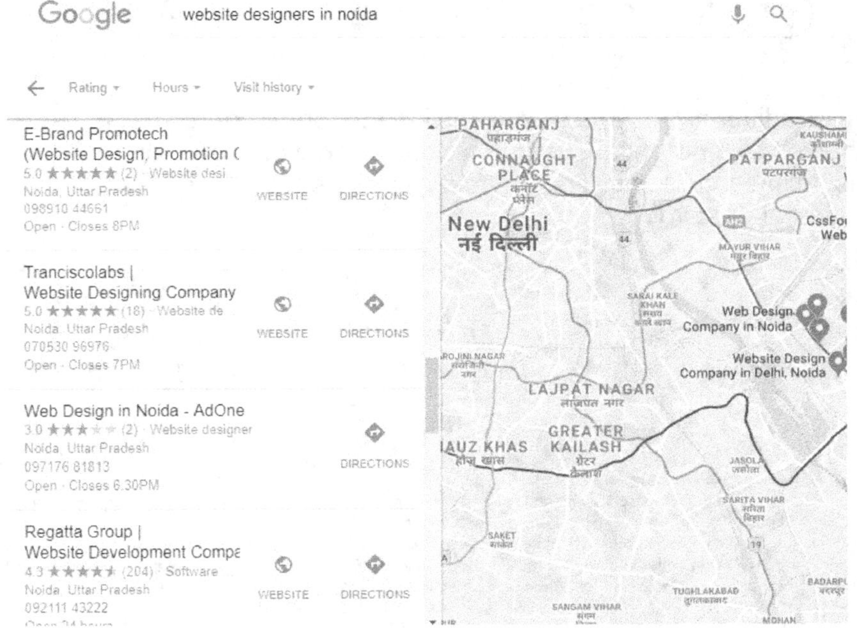

As you can see in the image above a site with more than 204 reviews is way below in search results.
Some common reasons for sites that have more reviews but are ranking below:-

1. All the reviews are by people who have not done reviews in the past.
2. 90% of the reviews are done on a single day, and after that, no reviews are done. These reviews on your business were their first review.
3. Reviews are from countries where our business does not give services. This is an example of purchasing reviews.

4. Reviews have been done from the same location.

Percentage of Negative Reviews responded.

How you respond to negative reviews, shows everything about your company, its values, and culture inside out. While replying to a particular situation, try to be in customer shoes. Feel how he would have felt after being dissatisfied with your product or service.

In a traditional world, one dissatisfied customer could affect the choices of 4 potential customers, but in a digital world, one dissatisfied customer could affect decisions of more than 400 potential customers.

R G
Local Guide · 76 reviews · 34 photos

★ ☆ ☆ ☆ ☆ 3 months ago

No sound absorbing materials, extremely loud. Party groups right next to people trying to dine. Fish the size of a thick cell phone battery. Good flatbread pesto. Excellent cinnamon ice cream. But never again.

 Like

Response from the owner 3 months ago
While it's great the ice cream and flatbread pesto impressed you, I'm sorry if your experience could've been better. If you had any preferences with the seating, we would've been happy to accommodate if something else had been available. We are a Tavern but we do have an upstairs available for dining that is a little better on the ear. I hope you'll give us another chance so you can get the kind of excellent experience we're known for. -Bonni

It would help if you also tried to offer a solution to the problem, and most importantly, try your best to take the conversation offline. It will keep further discussion confidential, and that is positive for your business.

At last, give your email address too if you think a customer has faced hardships using your product. Alternatively, provide your phone number also if you believe the review is fake.

Social Listings

Social listing refers to having a listing on all the Social Media, where you can manage your online brand. LinkedIn, Twitter, and Facebook sometimes outranks your website and appear much higher in the seach results.

This is because indexing of these social websites is done way faster than your website.

6.3 Advanced Terminologies

City Specific Landing Page

It refers to having a different page on the website as well as Google My Business Listing. Let's take an example of Columbia Asia Hospitals. They have a separate website page as well as Google My Business listing for every business.

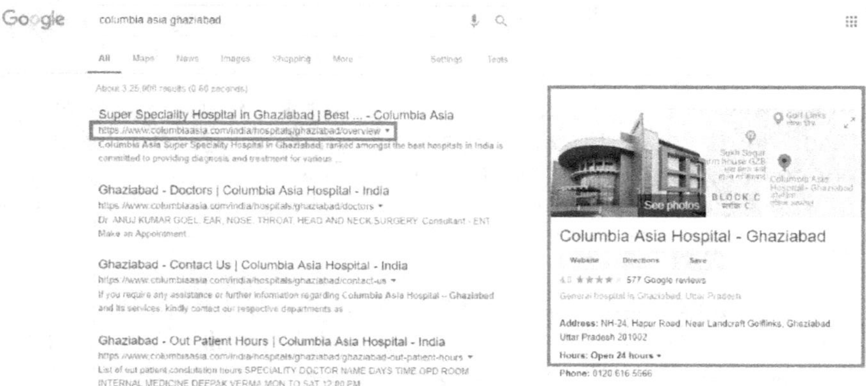

As we can see in the image above, Columbia Asia has different website pages for all the franchises all over India and also a new Google My Business page where customer can leave reviews on their experience in the hospital of that local city.

If you offer services that expand to more than one city, you should definitely experiment with city specific landing page.

Structured Data Markup

Structured Data permits web crawlers to creep your webpage understanding every minute detail of what is there on your website. Everything is HTML code to them but pieces of content as address, name of author, book or describing what that code means is using structured data.

To understand how the individual elements of the webpage are marked via schema, you can visit https://schema.org.

 A few components that appear to be flawlessly evident to us people are pointless to web crawlers. That is the place organized information comes in to play. Organized information is added legitimately to a page's HTML markup. Web indexes utilize related information to produce rich bits, which are little snippets of data that will at that point, show up in list items.

Structured Data is essential for SEO because it'll make it easier for Google to understand what your pages and your website are about. Above that, structured data markup will change the way your search results will look like. It'll show more information to your customer or more specific information. And this will increase the likelihood a customer will click on your results. More clicks will eventually lead to even higher rankings.

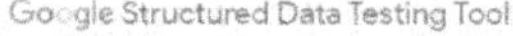

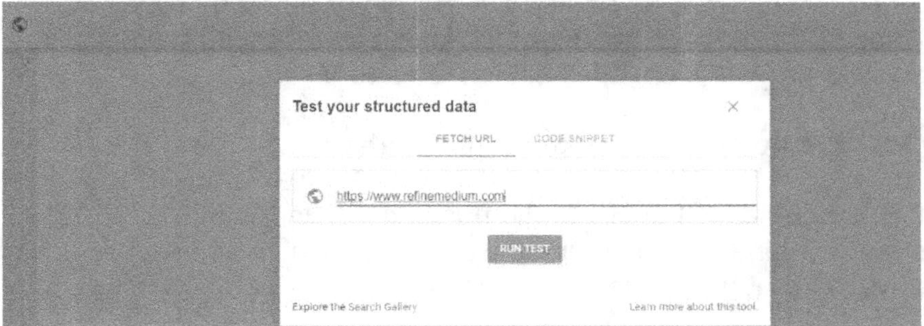

To check whether your website has Structured Data Markup, you can search "Google Structured Data Testing Tool."

Link: https://search.google.com/structured-data/testing-tool/u/0/

Google My Business ads convert well.

Along with a high click-through rate, Google My Business ads have a very high conversion rate. We have seen CTR of 16.40% for the clients, but the average that you can expect is 6%.

This shows that Google My Business lists are handy and have a high click-through rate as compared to other forms of advertisement.

Localized Content

Localization went beyond directly modifying a translation to make it local. Nowadays, it is vital that your product and content sound authentic in the locale you are targeting. Localization creates a connection that enhances the value of your product for consumers.

Also consumers feel confessed that the ability to obtain information in their language was more important than the price.

So, if you can use the regional language of your area,
 This can give your business a competitive edge, expand your market, avoid liability, and create a distinctive brand around the world. So try to keep the focus on localization when creating content for your local business on Google My Business.

On Page Location Keyword Optimization

It is concerned with using *schemas* to mark your content. To tell search engines about your local address, local business, or anything that geo targets your market.

If your content belongs to a particular city then use schemas to mark them.

Check schema.org website to see how you can mark every form of your content.

Example 2

Without Markup   Microdata   RDFa   JSON-LD

```
<h1>Disneyland Paris</h1>
<div>It's an amusement park in Marne-la-Vallée, near Paris, in France.</div>
<div>Hours: Mo-Fr 10am-7pm Sa 10am-22pm Su 10am-21pm</div>
<div>Entrance: with ticket</div>
<div>Currency accepted: Euro</div>
<div>Payment accepted: Cash, Credit Card</div>
<div>Website:
      <a href="http://www.disneylandparis.it/">www.disneylandparis.it</a>
</div>
```

Quick Access to:
Local Business Schema: https://schema.org/LocalBusiness
Place Schema: https://schema.org/Place
Restaurant Schema: https://schema.org/Restaurant
Address Schema: https://schema.org/address
Opening Hours Schema: https://schema.org/openingHours

6.4 Local Backlinks

Backlinks play a vital role in the ranking of a website. And when your potential prospects are virtually worldwide, the traditional thought process would be to have as many authoritative domains as possible to refer to your sites for a better Google ranking. However, this strategy may not be as relevant for a website that depends solely on local buyers.

Local Directory Websites

Search for "Directories in [Local City]" and make your account in all of them. Make sure your Name, Address, and Phone Number is uniform in all of them. If you change your Name, Address or phone number slightly then Google sees this as a separate listing.

Local Partner Sites

Local partner sites are the sites which help the site grow. Let's take the example of any business; if there is more than one owner of a company, then they are partners. Similarly, in this case, the local partner sites are the sites which are referring people to our website and help us grow. It can be two independent business too.

Local Newspaper Sites

Newspaper backlinks are the most trustworthy when seen from a search engine point of view because news sites represent authenticity. Even two quality backlinks can outrank your competition with thousands of backlinks.

Search for: "Newspapers in [Local City]," "Online News in [Local City]," "Epaper in [Local City]"

Industry Specific Sites

Industry-specific sites refer to the business that belongs to the same industry as yours. Now the question is why they would give you backlinks? **Organize an event with them**. Google does not understand the content. It recognizes that the other business now recommends you. This form of backlinks even outranks backlinks from news sites.

Local Bloggers

 Common sites are static where content is not updated as often as possible. While a blog is dynamic, and it is generally crawled more times than a static website. So next time you are planning an event that needs immediate search rankings. Contact local bloggers in your community. When we talk about local bloggers, the area of search can expand from town to city to state in case of bloggers only. Quality bloggers are less in number, so we contact state or national bloggers.

Search for following terms to find Bloggers

"Bloggers in [Local City]," "Bloggers in [Nearby City]," "Bloggers in [Your Industry]," "Bloggers in [Your Business]"

Local Charities

Local charities are the NGOs nearby that operate in your area. Getting backlinks from them is the easiest and authoritative. Easy as any association requires a little help from your side in monetary form or any sort of voluntary aid, and they will give you the backlinks. Authoritative as these NGOs and trusts are generally covered by national news sites or regional news sites which makes the backlinks for your business much valuable.

Search for following to find "Local Charities."
"NGOs in [Local City]," "Trusts in [Local City]," " Organ Donation NGOs in [Local City],"

You might find a state government website with links to all the registrations.

Host Local Events

Hosting a local event could get you covered by news and network site. They even foster industry partnerships.

Neighborhood news and network sites in your city frequently post news for nearby occasions. Besides, these kinds of news and network sites are regularly indexed and have high authority in terms of Search Engines.

Conclusion

When we talk about Local SEO, we have to think in terms of geographical location of the business and make sure that business is "Google My Business" verified which shows Google that they are located nearby. The more local links you get, higher are the chances for you ranking for nearby searches.

7. Link Building

Link building is when you work to acquire hyperlinks that link from someone else's website to yours. The process exists necessarily to allow the exchange of links to increase the number of quality backlinks your site holds. Hyperlinks or links are used for navigation around the internet, and they're used by search engines to crawl the web. Successfully promoting your content requires good online rankings, and improving your rankings requires good backlinks. So, it's highly recommended that you polish your link building skills and get on board with the emerging link building trends.

You cannot rank without links and gone are the days where you could rank with weaker content. Your content needs to be flawless. The strategy mentioned below might not work if you are optimizing a low-quality article.

A Change in Traditional Link Building Techniques

Traditional link building used to rely on simple and straightforward methods of asking for links. Now it's a combination of a bunch of marketing strategies. Google's algorithms are continually evolving and becoming more complex. They consistently adjust their algorithms according to the behavior of users and have become highly adaptive to cater to more specific search requirements. Since link building techniques are so tightly integrated with search engine optimization tactics, link building needs to evolve with Google's algorithms.

Link building used to consist of the least amount of personalization and content while widely implementing black hat techniques. Those techniques soon fell out of practice due to Google's algorithm improvements. Nowadays, more focus is on actually earning the links and building beneficial relationships within your community. The standard of link building has leveled up drastically due to improvements in Google's scrutinizing strategies.

7.1 Link Building Ways

Link building ways consist of all the basics that need to be covered to get your blog up and running. Remember link building is about quality and not quantity of links.

Let us get going:-

Link Reclamation

This is a straightforward method for starting your link building strategy since you don't have to build the links, rather fix the old, broken ones.

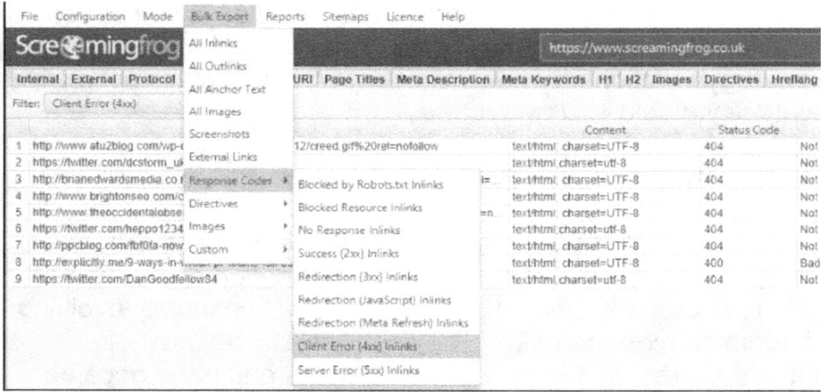

Check your website for all the 404 errors via Screaming Frog software and fix those errors.

Apart from cleaning 404 errors, you can also opt for reclaiming image links by using tools such as Tineye.com which will help in searching the web if your image is used.

Email Outreach

Email outreach can significantly help in building substantial links. However, there's one primary concern: How do you successfully reach out to others and not end up with their spam emails? Do not use terms like offer, discount, money or deals.

The first step is to search for likely linkers or people that are most likely to link to you.

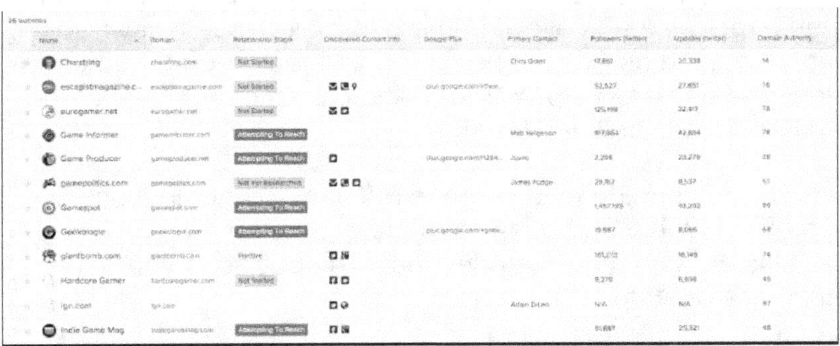

Before presenting your offer on the email, make sure that the offer is something that you love and it would take some effort to make it. When you contact bloggers that have a following of 2000-5000. Use a tracking software like Mailtrack to see when your emails are read.

Guest Blogging

Guest posts increase your brand awareness and SEO authority. If you can manage to post at multiple locations at once, it would appear that you are everywhere.

However, you should not contact everyone you search for guest blogging opportunities. Keep these criteria while contacting the website.
-Domain Authority of 45+.

- Credit to Guest Bloggers with their Bio.
-Site traffic, page views, and reach.
-Social Following of 10,000+.
-Target audience is similar.

Remember to have the link of a landing page in author bio instead of your homepage. This would increase conversions for your newsletter.

Directories

When was the last time you used a directory to go to a business? Yes, we use a search engine. However, still, directories help you create a profile with valuable links. The key is to find relevant and targeted directories and allowing them to make you discoverable on platforms such as Facebook or Google Maps. Some of the top directories to use are Yelp, Yellow Pages, Best of The Web, Map Quest, Facebook, Justdial, Sulekha.

Remember, registering in directories relevant to your industry is much more valuable and apart from the generic ones mentioned above. Also, search for directories that are specific to your particular city or state.

Link Worthy Content

Creating link worthy content is one of the best ways to increase buzz about your brand. The key is to gather trending content and connect it with your specific brand. More than 71.4% of marketers are focused on creating content. Quality content gets you backlinks. Simple formula.

Consider partnering with another brand as a co-author in an article and before even proceeding, have a mutual understanding to do some paid promotion where you both pay equal in your specific social channels.

Content Syndication

Content Syndication means to post your content on other sites like LinkedIn and Medium, to increase the visibility of the content across platforms.

Whenever you are using content syndication make sure rel=canonical tag is added, and you are adding a nofollow tag as well.

You can syndicate your content on the following sites:-

1.LinkedIn
2. Quora
3. Stumbleupon
4. Facebook
5.Yahoo
6.Slideshare
7.Tumblr
8. Medium

Content syndication increases your overall website authority and increases your backlinks for that specific article.

Blog Comments

Comments add value and engage people even though they are a tad bit more work than the other link building methods.

 For successful blog commenting, you need to find high-quality websites with competent domain authority of over 60+ and article that are most relevant to your target audience. Whenever you are commenting, always refer to the author by name and make sure to engage with other users and the most important is to add value in the comment and infallibility end the comment with a compliment. Keep comments under 100 words.

Brand Mentions

The only way of getting links without any hard work is monitoring brand mentions. Five parameters are monitored while we create alerts

-Keyword Alert
- Brand Alerts
-Domain Alerts
-Author Alerts
-Link Alerts

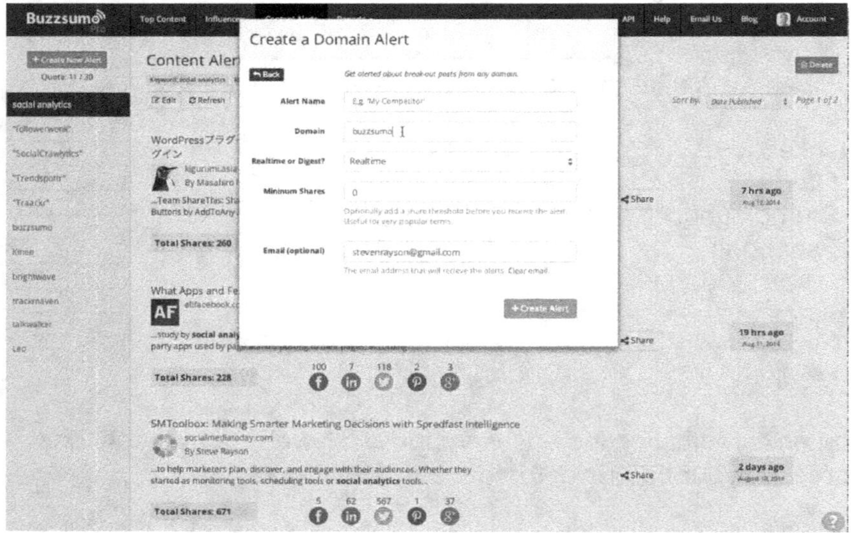

 If anyone in the community uses factors that you want to track, then you will immediately get an email regarding it. The above image is of Buzzsumo brand monitoring tool. (Free solution: Google Alerts)

Conclusion

Link building is not magic. For any of the procedure to show some significant results, wait for at least 3-4 months before trying out new strategies.

There may be a temptation to try out blackhat tools for some quick results since they promise significant outputs in no time. This is where you have to understand that when we talk about SEO and linkbuilding, there is no overnight ranking. It always takes time for websites to rank.

8. Technical SEO

Technical SEO is means optimizing website, server, and blog and tweak it so that search engines could better crawl and index our site which leads to improved organic rankings.

<noscript for javascript>

Use a <noscripttag> for content that is contained in Javascript. Make sure that is there in the script is the same.

```
<script type="text/javascript">
document.write("Out of sight, out of mind")
</script>
<noscript>Out of sight, out of mind</noscript>
```

Disable Javascript in your browser to check results.

Hosting with reliable servers:

It costs only a handful of bucks to get a 24/7 technical assistance from the hosting provider. Before choosing any hosting provider, take a cpanel demo.

A wrong hosting provider can cost you in countless ways. A slow site is frustrating for your customers and your readers. However, apart from readers point of view, your site ranking can also reduce in the search results as site speed is an essential factor.

Other factors you can consider while choosing any hosting provider are.
- Technical support.

- Add-ons that they provide like "One click Wordpress Install."
-The user interface of the Control Panel.
-Account Suspension cases and scenario.
- Customer reviews.

For small projects, you can experiment with anything as the cost does not matter, but for significant projects, consider purchasing a good hosting.

Cookies

Do you know cookies are the reason behind the advertising business of Google generating more than 20 billion dollars approx annually? Whatever you visit on the web like say a blog or a coffee restaurant or any ecommerce site, Google will serve you advertisements based on your interest and if ads are served based on your interest, then you might be interested in the ads that are being offered.

After some organizations and individuals sued Google on tracking user cookies, now it displays a message that this website uses cookies to give the most relevant results. Results mean advertising business of Google.

Now the only thing that you can do is to customize the message so that it represents your brand. Else Google will display an automatic message, and people are used to reading these template messages.

Ask your designer to develop a custom message. Remember that every chance to be different on the website is a chance to leave a mark on the visitor so that your voice is remembered.

Content Distribution Network

Let's say you have a website hosted on a Chinese server in China and a request is coming from Sri Lanka. When a user pings the server, it will take more time in loading the site.

CDN will ensure that the time taken from around the globe is nearly the same as it is to your local server in the opening of your website. It means if your local server is hosted in India and it takes around 2 seconds to load the site, then the same amount of time will be required for a user in China because he will be pinging the server in China not in India as it will take more time in loading the website.

Now, whenever you purchase any hosting package, shoot an email to enquire regarding this service. Like Bluehost offers this service with its hosting package but its plan differs from country to country. So whenever you purchase hosting from any company, start your investigation asking about CDN or Content Distribution Network.

Do you know every 1-second delay costs more than 1 billion in sales for Amazon yearly?

Siloing

The purpose of siloing is to organize all the data in such a way that the related webpages are together piled up in a page or a place.

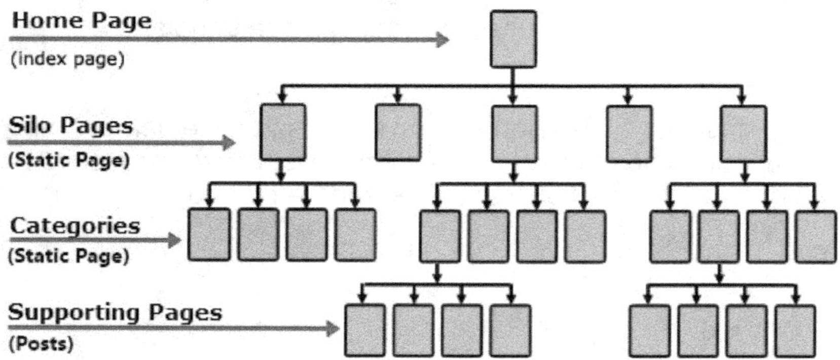

A good silo structure allows search engines to easily explore your site and understand the relationships between pages, creating a more targeted database entity for your website around each topic. With the solid silo in place, every page of your site will get a considerable amount of internal link juice buildup - as it is grouped and connected to other similar pages.

Broken Links Prevention

Broken links can be observed if a website server is unavailable, webpage is outdated, site is shifted to a new domain or the page has been removed.

If a link remains broken for a longer period of time, it shows the search engine that website has gone outdated and your organic rank starts decreasing.

Discovering the links that are broken is difficult but automation tools have made it easier. Check the broken links of your website from "Screaming Frog" or www.deadlinkchecker.com.

Friendly URLs

A friendly URL accurately describes the page using easy-to-read keywords for search engines and users. Give humans and crawlers a good sign of the nature of the page. The URL is also shown in the search results, and well-designed URLs are more useful and more appealing to users, which mean higher click rates.

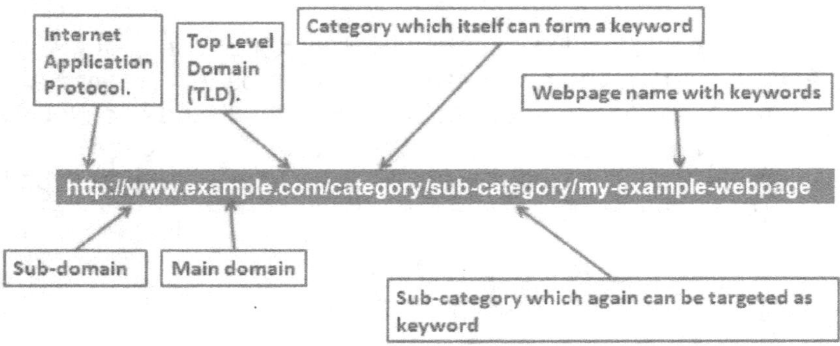

Mark Up the Content

The tags must be put in better HTML elements for the textual content in a page. Keeping this in mind, all the webpages must be pertinent to the content. After managing the backlinks and anchor texts, the marking up the content is the most useful thing to aid the crawler to relate the documents with the web content.

Let's start with an example. Let's say that your webpage is about movie Avatar - a page with a link to a trailer, information about the director, etc. Your HTML code might look something like this:

```
<div>
 <h1>Avatar</h1>
 <span>Director: James Cameron (born August 16, 1954)</span>
 <span>Science fiction</span>
 <a href="../movies/avatar-theatrical-trailer.html">Trailer</a>
</div>
```

Initially, recognize the category of the webpage that concerns the movie Avatar. To do this, add the itemscope element to the HTML tag containing information about the element, as follows:

```
<div itemscope>
  <h1>Avatar</h1>
  <span>Director: James Cameron (born August 16, 1954) </span>
  <span>Science fiction</span>
  <a href="../movies/avatar-theatrical-trailer.html">Trailer</a>
</div>
```

By adding itemscope, you indicate that the HTML contained in the <div> ... </ div> block is for a particular element.

However, it is not very useful to specify that an item is being discussed without specifying what kind of item it is. You can specify the item type by using the item type attribute immediately after item scope.

```html
<div itemscope itemtype="http://schema.org/Movie">
  <h1>Avatar</h1>
  <span>Director: James Cameron (born August 16, 1954)</span>
  <span>Science fiction</span>
  <a href="../movies/avatar-theatrical-trailer.html">Trailer</a>
</div>
```

This specifies that the elements contained in the div are a movie, as defined in the schema.org type hierarchy. Element types are provided as URLs, in this case, http://schema.org/Movie.

Check all the schema at https://schema.org/.

Heatmap

Heatmap is the sections of the website where users interact the most. Doing a Heatmap testing will give you an idea to place your essential stuff in the area where people spend time.
F Letter – People scan your website in F shape. So value should be provided considering this user behavior.

The Heatmap testing tool that you can try is Crazyegg and Heatmap.me.

Structured Data

Structured data as a universal term which denotes to all organized data. For example, if you have a multitude of posts which note scattered information with phone messages about meetings, dates, times, people, etc., and arrange them in a table with rows and columns labeled for each type of information, then it is known as structuring the data.

A. Example of unstructured data

1: "Michael called, confirming 3 pm on Wednesday at the cafe."
2: "Do not forget your 10 am meeting at Mary's office this Friday."

B. Example of structured data

Meeting With	Date	Time	Location

Meeting With	Date	Time	Location
Michael	Wednesday	3 pm	Coffee Shop
Mary	Friday	10 am	Office

Avoid Cloaking

Cloaking is a procedure for carrying a specific set of webpages to search engine crawlers, while at the same time offering a completely different set of pages to your human visitors.

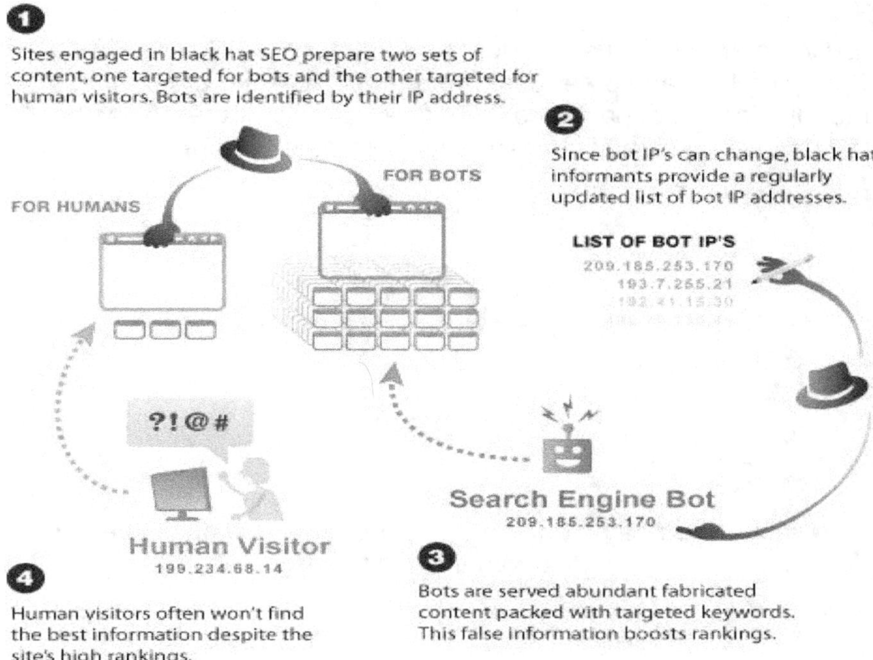

It is generally done to trick search engines into giving higher rankings to web pages.

Canonicalization

Canonicalization means when a Website offers the same content on different links. As you can see in the image below the Amazon homepage opens when you type their website and also when you come via email or bots.

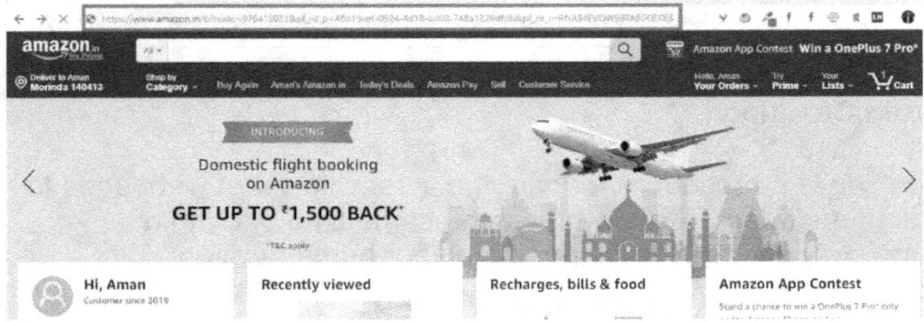

E-Commerce website categorizes webpages via Session IDs, Shopping IDs, and other user parameters so there are chances that duplication of pages could happen. So we put rel="canonical" tag or if we have multiple page then rel="next" and rel="prev".

```
<link rel="canonical"
href="http://www.example.com/article?story=abc&page=2"/>

<link rel="prev"
href="http://www.example.com/article?story=abc&page=1&sess
ionid=123" />

<link rel="next"
href="http://www.example.com/article?story=abc&page=3&sess
ionid=123" />
```

This shows the search engine that your content is duplicate across domains and not to index domains individually.

Code for Speed

Speed is the most crucial factor which affects the rank of the websites in search engines. First, before optimizing your website, check its speed from "webpagetest.org," "yslow" or "Google Page speed insights."

Even a 1-second delay in loading your website can decrease its conversion by more than 10%. People will close the website if it is taking too much time to load. Google these days ranks a website based on its speed. So, faster your website is more chances that you show at the top of their search results.

National Train Enquiry System -Indian Railways

enquiry.indianrail.gov.in

⚠ Slow to load - Official Indian Railways site for travelers using railways for taking holiday vacation trips, official trips, tours, and daily commute.

As you can see in the image, Google also displays "Slow to Load" message below the domain of the website. So people will surely not click if this message is displayed while they are searching for your website.

Correct all the flaws by Google PageSpeed Insights and check after you clear your cache. Don't try to achieve 100/100 on desktop and mobile. Anything above 85 is good.

A significant boost in website speed can be achieved if you can "Minify HTTP Requests" and by using "Content Delivery Networks".

"Nofollow Links"

'Nofollow' links mean that we are saying to search engines not to follow the links that are marked nofollow. To make a link nofollow we mark it with rel=nofollow like

<a href =www.abc.com rel="nofollow"> My website </a>

 Opposite of nofollow is dofollow it means that the link should be followed. Suppose two teachers are teaching Mathematics. One has 120 students, whereas the other has no students. There might be reasons like the Teachers is new, but what we take into consideration is the popularity amongst the students as it is a social indicator that the teacher is good at his profession. And this is how Google even takes into consideration the links flowing towards a site.

In today's era, each teacher is having some equal no of students (Backlinks). So how do we judge the teacher? It is by the quality of his students and by the overall result. In terms of web, the quality of students means the quality of backlinks and overall effect mean the bounce rate, social popularity, and web shares.

Robot.txt

Robot.txt is a file that search engines use to see information related to a particular website. Now before indexing web page of any website, search engines first check the robot.txt of that website to see if there is any page that is not to be indexed and it can be done by using *disallow.*

This is how we can put disallow into practice.

1. Disallowing Temporary folder:

*User-agent: **
Disallow : /tmp/

2.If we want no search engine bot to access our website, then this can be done by:

*User-agent: **
Disallow:/

3. To prevent some specific URL from being indexed:

*User-agent: **
Disallow : /aman/personal/

In the third example, the URL will look like www.mywebsite.com/aman/personal/. All the information related to the robot.txt file can be found at *robottxt.org.*

Redirects 301

301 redirect means forwarding a URL to a different URL or domain. Now let's say we have a domain xyz.com and whenever a person opens 'xyz.com' he is redirected to 'abc.com' which is our new site. This is 301 redirect where a domain is redirected to a different domain.

301 redirect can also exist with URL parameters of the same domain like xyz.com/posts/paintings-walls/ is redirected to xyz.com/posts/paiting-walls-basics-101/

301 redirect tells the search engines that this page is shifted to a new page and to pass the rankings it gave to the old page to the redirected page as both have collaborated.

Traffic Loads

If you are working on a major project, then you should check the traffic load that your website can take. When you check for the traffic loads, you might have to change your hosting provider, as most of the promises about the site speed and the load that it can bear are unleashed as we check the speed and it is undoubtedly better than website crashing.

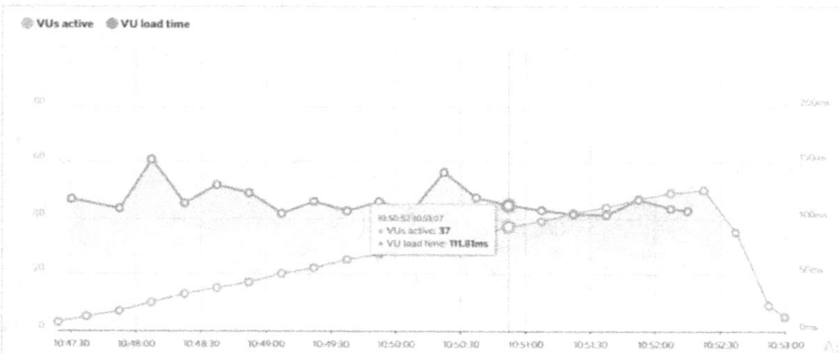

Above test was done on a paid tool named Loadimpact (Free Tool-Apache Jmeter). VU stands for Virtual Users, and the screenshot says that when there were 37 users active, then the load time was 111.81ms, which is pretty fast as the test was done for a local cupcake factory.

Browser Behavior

Different browsers tend to behave differently, and it is essential to test for things like Screen size, JavaScript, or whether or not your plugins are working well across all platforms. Checking manually for all the browsers can make the task tedious for the developers.

Here comes *browsershots .org* to the rescue.

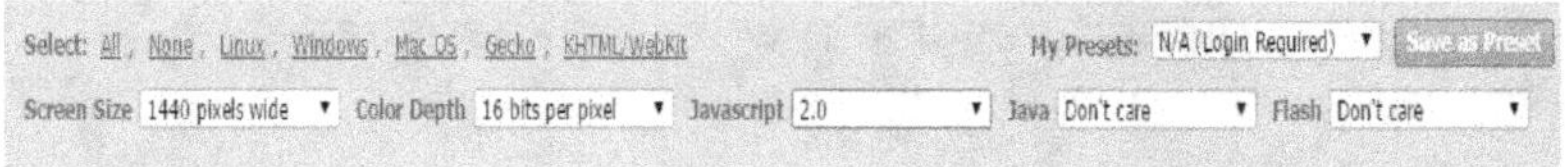

All you have to do is select the browsers that you want to test. It is a good idea to choose all and proceed, as shown in the image below.

You can also customize things like operating system and elements like screen size, color depth, and flash to test for specific aspects of your website.

WAI-ARIA

WAI stands for web accessibility initiative, and ARIA stands for accessible rich internet application suite. Blind man needs a stick to walk, and to read a book Braille is used where a person gets the feel of the alphabet by touching but what about the Internet? Are screen readers enough?

No, they are not. There is no way a person can know that image with dog food is an advertisement, yes there are tags that display that a particular block is an advertisement but how much percent of people abide by the rules so that people with disability could read on their site?

Imagine a person with a disability reading a story, and suddenly he is greeted with a popup that says Sign up to receive free updates when he signs up, he is redirected to another offer that says it is going to expire soon. I mean, can you imagine the frustration that these people have while they read on the web?

Since the concept of WAI-ARIA is relatively new as it was started around March 2014. It will certainly take time for developers around the world to get adapted to it. However, the guidelines are pretty simple to follow and can be accessed at 'www.*w3.org/wai.*' In simple words, WAI-ARIA is meant for people with disabilities so that their reading experience could be better.

Conclusion

Technical SEO does not stop here. It starts with these guidelines. It is also not a onetime process; it needs to be done regularly. The website needs to be checked for the above precept regularly.

Next time you design and develop a website, keep these parameters as a checklist.

9.Advanced Blog Optimization

Advance blog optimizations are the tactics and methodologies that will take your significant amount of time, but when executed, your content will be evergreen on the search engine result pages.

Although you should generally give priority to writing for your audience rather than for search engines, Here are some ways where you can take care of both users and search engines:

9.1 Complete Content:

Let's start with some history. During 2009, On-Page SEO was straightforward to do so as compared to today. It was a combination of 3 easy steps:

1. Writing the content of your article
2. Adding some keywords
3. Publishing your article or blog

And voila your piece is ready. Although you can still write articles through this outdated method and get traffic, it's not the best method to generate users on your blog post anymore. To get your position on the first page of top search engines like Google and Bing, you need to provide such content that covers the entire concept of your content in-depth.

Recently during an interview, Google's John Mueller was asked, why some of their pages weren't getting indexed. He replied: "You can generally make the quality of the content there a little bit better by having more comprehensive content on these pages."

To show Google that your content is comprehensive, it should contain "Subtopic Terms" in your content, and when Google sees Subtopic Terms on your page, they're much more likely to consider it comprehensive.

For example, let's say that you just published an article about a cartoon named 'The Simpsons.' However, for Google to consider it a complete content article, it must consist of subtopic terms like:

Homie Homer
Marge
Ned
Krusty, The Clown

And when they see Subtopic terms like these, they will see that this content completely covers every aspect of the Simpsons in depth. Moreover, when you give Google what it demands, you can expect your content to be promoted to a higher ranking on the search engine.

To get subtopic terms on Google, you need to search your keyword on Google Images and the suggestions below should be included as subtopic terms.

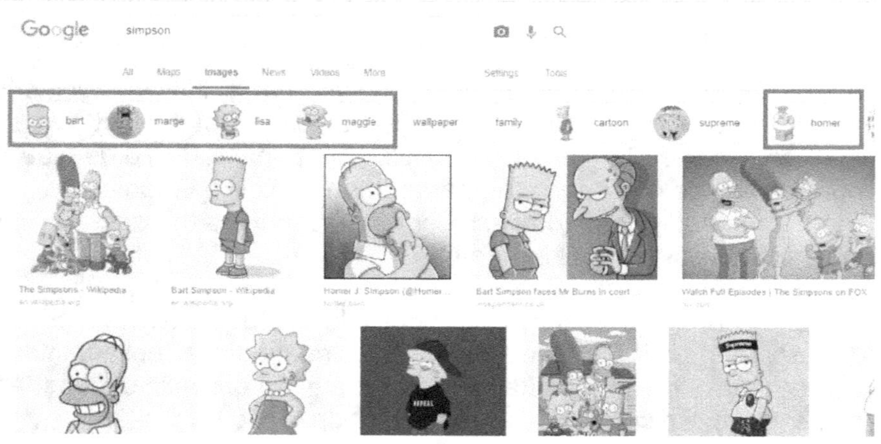

This is one of the best methods to ensure Google that your content is complete, and it will help you rank your post in the top pages.

9.2 Expert Roundup Posts

An expert roundup is a group of interviews by prominent people in your niche. Each contributor should be someone with some authority in your field, and that has something to add to your readers.

The most operative roundups pose an exact question that the experts can respond to. It should be a question that people care about.

Here are a few examples of titles of roundup posts:

-55 SEO Experts reveal their Favorite Tools
-80 Productivity Tips from Incredibly Busy Experts

To have these roundup posts up and running, this is the methodology that you should follow:

First: Figuring out what is the right question.

The first and most important thing that you need to figure out is what is the simple query and topic for your roundup post. Questions should be such that they should give answers to problems statements that are relevant and crisp.

If you are unable to understand that what might be a spectacular query or question, you can utilize tools like "Ahrefs" or "Buzzsumo."

For Instance, this is an example for searching the keyword 'remote work' on Ahref:

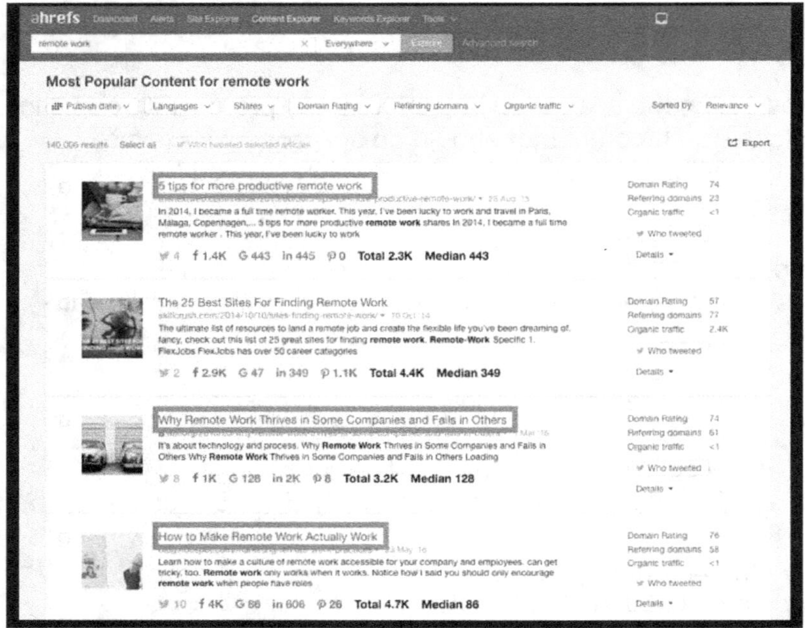

- For instance, the first article is about how you can productively work more remotely. You can make an excellent round-up question using the first article. With this in mind, have a roundup post like "85 Experts reveal their strategy of working remote."

- Expert tip: Whatever topic or question you have chosen to make it as simple and easy as possible for your experts to answer, the question should be precise and to the point and should be explained in layman's term.

Furthermore: Find the correct specialists

Your specialists are likely going to be contained, bloggers and advertisers. On the off chance that you've been working in your specific specialty for some time, you ought to have a sensibly smart thought about who the specialists are. The exceptional the names that you can pull in, the more fruitful your content is probably going to be. This is because their investment adds authenticity to your article.

Also after the blog post is published each expert shares it to their Network which results in adding the value and marketing for you.

Thirdly: Collect master contact subtleties.

Start by making a spreadsheet to monitor names, messages, Twitter handles, and friends or blog URLs. Note: You can tailor the subtleties of your spreadsheet dependent on the sort of data you feel is imperative to monitor.

And Finally: Contact the specialists

It is expert opinion for you that you should contact your experts at least two times. Initially contact experts and then email them after two days as a reminder.

Use Email Tracking extension like Mailtrack to see when somebody read your email, how many times someone opened a particular email or from which device they are opening their email.

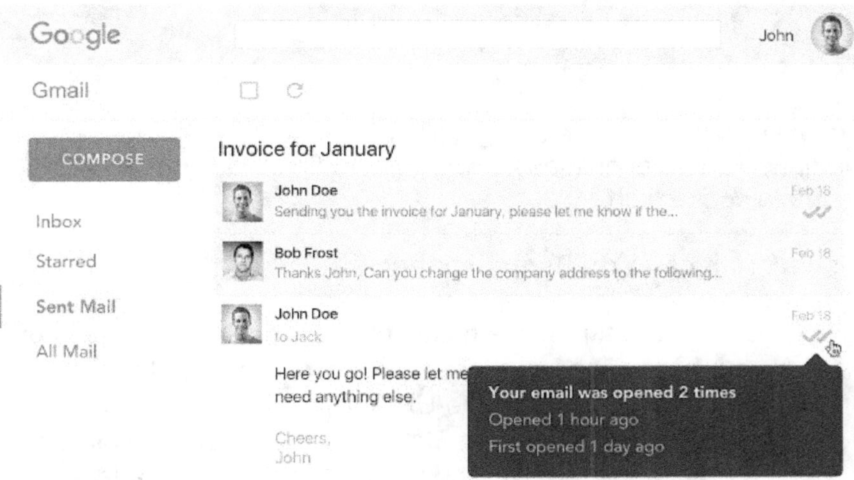

This type of tracking will help in directing your efforts towards people who are reading your email.

9.3 Internal Deep Linking

Deep linking refers to linking internal pages on the website to rank them as well on the search engine.

Category 1 gives us a suggestion to read about post 1. Post 1 provides us with a recommendation to read about post 2, and as we read about post 3, we are recommended to post 4. Browsing one page of the website, we are browsing more and more posts. This is internal linking. The more content people read on the blog; the more content will rank on search engine result pages.

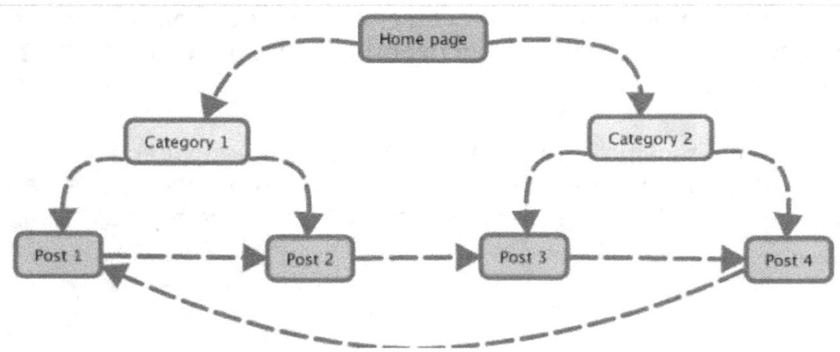

Deep links increase the navigability of the site, which engages the audience and makes it easier for them to find the information that leads to conversion.

Useful Tactics to do Deep Linking:

- Email signatures: It is quite common to put the address of your home page in a large amount of bio-type data. For example, you will put the URL of your homepage in the biography of your email. Do not do that. Instead, link to an internal page that will add value to your email readers.

- Guest posts: Another common tactic when it comes to linking to your home page is when you write a guest post. Usually, you will write something like "Aman Tandon is a ... and blogs in My blog", which links to your home page.

Instead, link to a deep page on your site that will direct traffic to a relevant page, thus reducing the number of rebounds you will get.

- Blog comments – It is quite natural that you leave the address of your home page in the website form on people's blogs when you leave a comment. A better strategy is to leave a link to an internal page that is relevant to that audience even it is a nofollow link.

- Forums: As with blog comments, if you leave a comment in a forum, be sure to manually enter a URL that will direct traffic to an internal page instead of your home page.

Link more and more internal pages instead of linking homepage, this will pass the link juice to your posts which ultimately means they will also start ranking.

9.4 Topic Clusters

Topic Clusters are a collection of articles or pages interrelated around a general theme. They allow you to provide greater visibility to search engines as it shows them that you have an extensive range of topics on this field.

What's Pillar Content?

A pillar page is the basis on which a group of topics is built in. It covers all parts of the problem on a single page, with space for more in-depth reports on blog posts from more detailed clusters that link to hyperlink to the pillar page.

What is Cluster Content?

A content group is a topic modeling structure in which the related content is "grouped" around a page of the central pillar. Establishing your content in this way can help Google understand the relationship between the pages, and build your authority around a topic, not just a single keyword. It will Increase search visibility and better return on investment from your content marketing efforts.

How does it work?

Traditionally there was a practice of building many posts for similar queries which led to our blog being repetitive. Cluster Content means linking the cluster so that even Bots know that there is a semantic relationship between them.

If you are Blogging about "A," it is your Pillar Content where are A.1 – A.2 –A.3 are your cluster content.

Pillar Content has the link to all the cluster, so "A" will have the links of A.1, A.2, A.3, and so on. Similarly, these clusters too will link back to Pillar Content Titled "A" and not between each other.

Topic Clusters show the search engines that you have a in-depth article around a topic and you are an authority figure on the subject.

9.5 Republish Old Blog Posts

If you have been blogging for a long time, you may feel that you are short of ideas as you have already covered many useful topics. Instead of struggling to find new ideas, republish old blog posts and look for the updates which users would love to read if it came to them. This will not only bring the old users to your site, but it will catch new users too.

Methods to Post Old Blog Posts:

1.   Adding updates & minor tweaks -

One of the best things about the new blog post is that you save a lot of writing time, which means you can put an extra effort in obtaining images, distributing your blog post, adding a PDF, GIF, and relevant resources.

Did you miss a typo for the first time? Are there errors in fact? Do you need to adjust some clumsy or confusing phrase? Let's say if you have posted about setting up a blog on some site, you may need to take new images and make sure that your step-by-step instructions are still accurate.

At last, lengthen your old blog posts to current trends.

2.   Rewrite old titles to be more SEO friendly-

While they may be titles that might not help your search engine rankings. The title of your blog is one of the most indispensable parts of your SEO facility, so if you want to rank higher in search engines, it is important to use titles that include your keywords and sound interesting enough to click. The best way to return to work titles? Try to think of the exact phrases that someone would look for to find your blog posts.

Republishing old blog posts generally means to update contents of post that might not be relevant to the user currently. This is also done so that efforts that were done previously in writing posts don't go to waste and it still add values to the users.

9.6 Broken Link Building via Wikipedia

Links coming from Wikipedia are considered to be very authentic and of high quality to search engines. Broken link building via Wikipedia is the art of finding Wikipedia pages where an external link is not working or is dead and instead put and suggest a link that point to our website. To defend this link, you need to have a very high-quality article on your website.

Beneath every Wikipedia page, we have "References" which point to external websites.

References [edit]

1. ^ Henry Mayhew: London Labour and the London Poor, 1861
2. ^ http://www.booth.lse.ac.uk (http://booth.ise.ac.uk/static/a/3.html) Charles Boot of the people in London (1886–1903) Archived July 26, 2014, at the Wayback Mac
3. ^ Meg Huby, Jonathan Bradshaw and Anne Corden 1999 A study of town life: living 100 years after Rowntree [dead link]
4. ^ http://www.columbia.edu (http://www.columbia.edu/acis/history/censustabulator.h Tabulator Archived May 14, 2008, at the Wayback Machine.
5. ^ *a b c* http://www.amsrs.com.au (http://www.amsrs.com.au/index.cfm?a=detail&ei Australian Market Research Retrieved Archived July 4, 2008, at the Wayback Mac
6. ^ July 2014 "Scientific Advertising" Check |url= value (help) (PDF).

In these Websites, some of these references are dead, and that is where our posts come into play.

Tool for finding broken links on Wikipedia: www.webfx.com/seo-tools/wikigrabber/

Enter the keyword that you want to rank for in the search option.

This is a rundown of pages on Wikipedia that needs fixing as they have a dead link. Click on the Wikipedia article and do CTRL+F to search "Dead Link" on the article.

Before giving your page as a link, make sure you have edited other articles as well, and the blog post that you are linking to is of very high quality.

9.7 Content for Questions

Question research allows you to understand natural language better. Asking a question triggers a natural answering reflex in human beings. Question optimization allows for increased organic search visibility of both featured snippets and Google's "People Also Ask" results. Lets begun:

1. Make question research part of keyword research

Serpstat uses Google's autosuggest results to produce the list of expressions based on your keywords.Once the list is spawned, you can click to the "Only Questions" tab to get lots of queries covering your keyword.

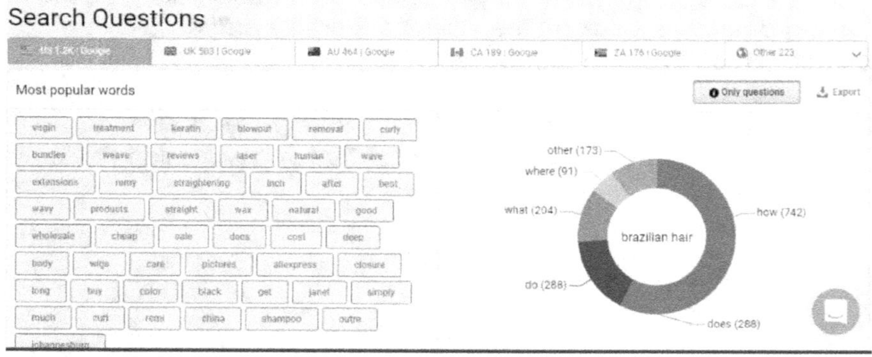

2.Using Quora

Go to Quora and type the keyword to get a suggestion or what are people around the globe asking:

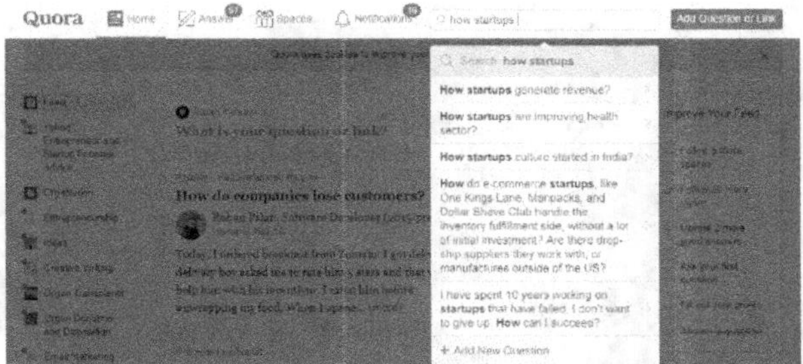

Keep typing individual letter after a keyword like "Why Startup a," "Why startup b" and do a comprehensive search. Also, while you are reading a question, you get similar suggestions of questions asked by other users. Take that too in the account.

Types of Questions

Direct Question

These question keywords start with "What," "Which," "Where," "Who," "When," and so on.

When the researcher asks a question such as "What is the name of our galaxy?" The intention is to obtain a direct answer, which in this case will be "The Milky Way."

what is the name of our galaxy

All   Images   News   Videos   Maps   More   Settings   Tools

About 58,60,00,000 results (0.87 seconds)

Milky Way

The term "**Milky Way**", a term which emerged in Classical Antiquity to describe the band of light in the night sky, has since gone on to become the name for our galaxy. Like many others in the known Universe, **the Milky Way** is a barred, spiral galaxy that is part of the Local Group – a collection of 54 galaxies.
Jul 28, 2017

What Is the Name Of Our Galaxy? - Universe Today
https://www.universetoday.com/74190/what-is-the-name-of-our-galaxy/

Short Questions

These questions begin with "Why".
When the researcher asks a question such as "Why is the ocean blue?" An answer snippet is returned.

Long Questions

When the researcher asks a question such as "How to cook pasta?" A step-by-step response is returned, in which the procedure is described. Here, the researcher intends to learn the method in the best possible way. Google accurately predicts user intent and returns search results that explain the process in several steps, as shown in the screenshot below:

> how to cook pasta

All   Videos   Images   Books   News   More   Settings   Tools

About 77,30,00,000 results (0.46 seconds)

Follow These Steps

1. **Boil** water in a large pot. To make sure **pasta** doesn't stick together, use at least 4 quarts of water for every pound of **noodles**.
2. Salt the water with at least a tablespoon—more is fine. The salty water adds flavor to the **pasta**.
3. Add **pasta**. ...
4. Stir the **pasta**. ...
5. Test the **pasta** by tasting it. ...
6. Drain the **pasta**.

How to Cook Pasta Video and Steps - Real Simple
https://www.realsimple.com/food-recipes/cooking-tips-techniques/cooking/cook-pasta

While you are doing Quora search, take all these three Types of question into account to get more specific queries and keywords for your posts.

9.8 Long Form Content

It may appear glaringly evident, yet there are various meanings of what long-form content genuinely is. A few people consider articles longer than 700 words to be long-structure, though others believe that articles must be more than 1,800 words to be viewed as long-structure.

Typically articles that have more than 3000 words are long-form content articles.

Step to Create Long-Form Content

1. Layout your Goals

For what reason would you like to make long-shape content?
Figure out what you're searching for. Would you like to construct brand mindfulness? Would you like to interface with your clients, develop your email list, get leads, or something different?
Your objectives will characterize how you execute the venture and will keep you responsible for deciding if it is a triumph.

Choose:
- Whom is your post for?
- Why are you composing it?
- What you will consider a triumph and how you will quantify it?
- Catchphrases and inquiry inquiries (What are individuals searching for?)
- Existing investigation (What content do you as of now have, perhaps on your blog that is performing great?)
- Target crowd (Whom are you following? What is most important to them? What do you think about them?)
- Rivalry (What else is out there? Would you be able to beat it?)
- Do it without anyone else's help or hire great writers.

That top quality may come at a high cost, however precise; good content is the contrast between blog posts that fly and blog posts that flops.

In case you're going to contact a specialist, ensure you furnish them with a clear framework. Fill them in on your objectives and get them familiar with your blog audience.

2. Choose Gated versus Ungated

Gated content implies that individuals need to fork over an email address (or other data) to download your book, while ungated means they can get to it unreservedly.

Blogging community generally vote in favor of ungated content because of the long haul estimation of having something open and sharable trumps a couple of email addresses as well.

3. Pick a Topic carefully

In case you're attempting to make sense of a point for a long-structure bit of substance, return to your objectives. Objective precedes theme. What sorts of issues will contact your gathering of people and support the action and conduct you're searching for?

Finally, when you are done with the above points, do the due research on the topic and post the content on the web.

10. SEO Strategy

An SEO strategy is organizing a website's content and pages in such a way so that each page is optimized for a particular group of keywords and interlinking of pages within a website is done in such a way that website starts ranking for even long tail keywords.

Mentioned below is one direction for ranking:

1.Competition: Before making an SEO strategy, do a technical audit of the competitor website to see its top competitors and where your website ranks compared to them.

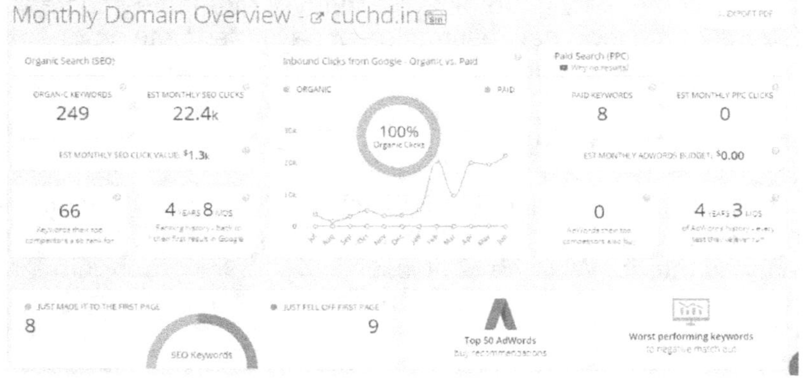

Use a tool like Spyfu to monitor every aspect of your competitor like where are they building backlinks from, where is the content shared, paid keywords, keywords that are ranking and a overall audit which will give you an idea of strong points of your competitors.

2. **Topic Research**: Make a list of topics that you would want to blog about, and they are related to your product or service. Initially keep the list up to 10-15 terms associated with your company.

Use Google Keyword Planner to see the search volume and competition for each keyword. Rank the list based on monthly search volume and relevance to your business.

3. **Make long tail keywords:** From the topics that you have shortlisted make long tail keywords from each topic. Let's say you have shortlisted college startups as one of the topics in the research then long tail keywords or blogs that I would want to post would be like

- Why College Startups Fail?
- Guide for College Startups before applying for Funding
-100 Mentors for College Startups who guide for Free- 50 Ways to get a customer for your College Startups

Fashion Make-Over					
	for your career	getting started	mistakes to avoid	celebrities	for relationships	saving money
how-to	- create a system - learn from others - impress your boss	- what you can do with $100 - clean the closet - create a budget	- impulse shopping - closet overwhelm	- what this celebrity did - less is best	- know what matters - 5 questions you can ask	- 10 ways to... - my experience - on-line resources
mistakes to avoid	- 7 ways to avoid... - wasting money	- avoiding over spending - mall disasters		- annual review of biggest...	- making it all about him/her	- 3 steps to take - what to avoid - annual review
trends	- careers and raises - research	- what to watch - what to not watch	- what we can learn from talk show hosts	- book review - top 10 changes	- less is best	- know what works - does it matter? - our survey
failure/success stories	- how I got started - mistakes I made	- what you can learn from the Oscars	- wasting money on...	- how I blew $1000 - how I saved $1000	- how one person...	- how this professional...
product reviews	- our fav. magazines	- how to choose...	- shoes	- opinion web sites - digital accessories	- on-line apps	- the 10 best accessories
opinion	- it's up to you - it doesn't matter	- we over think this	- why all fashion magazines are wrong - who to stop following - the secret behind...	- what Oprah knows - why all celebrities are wrong	- men vs. women - dating	- lies your mother told you
inspirational	- how to start small - even if you hate fashion	- tiny wins	- don't beat yourself up	- you don't have to	- best advice I got - what really matters	- what you can do on $10/month

The above is a outline of a Fashion Make-over blog. For each topic make at least 15 such posts.

4. **Blogging and Pages for each topic:** For each of the topics above make individual pages that link to your blog posts. Read subchapter "Internal Linking" and "Topic Clusters" in Advanced Blog Optimization.

5. **How frequently to update?** —Well, it is said to blog regularly so that your pages get indexed quickly in the search engine results. But you have to define what is regular for you. It can be daily, three days or weekly. As you decide what can be your blogging

frequency stick to it so that your readers know when to come back. As we blog regularly, our pillar content gets stronger in search results, which increases the chances of getting ranked in the search results.

Make an editorial calendar with date of posting of each blog post and also to the category of pillar content that it belongs to.

6. **Link Building Plan**: It generally refers to how and where your content will be shared. Now do not make heroic strategies to distribute the content everywhere. You can start small by sharing the content on social networks and make a strategy where your audience exists. Baby steps would look like:-

- Answering people on Quora with your blog posts
-Commenting at other blog posts with similar intent.
- Sending emails to subscribers, advertising your blog posts
-Contacting influencers that have identical topics to share your content with their audience.
-Contacting bloggers to add your content as a reference point.

It lucidly means the sources where your content should be shared over the web. Devote twice time in link building than it took you to write the post.

7. **Measure Everything**: How do you know if your content is successful or not? It does not depend on the total number of views of the blog post. Let's say you have written a blog post so that people could subscribe to your newsletter. Even if 60000 people have read your blog post in one hour and not a single subscription has happened to your newsletter, then it is not a successful

campaign.

Measure things like
- The total number of shares.
-Which medium attracted users?
-How many subscriptions happened from that blog post?
-The total number of views.
-Bounce rate from that post.
-The average time a person spends on the blog post.

When you quantify things, you will be able to make small tweaks that will bring you significant results.

Conclusion

This is the magic that would lead to consistent results, which will lead to more sales of your product. While you are making a strategy remember the following points:-

- Keep doing a technical audit of your website to know issues and ranking factors that might affect how crawlers scan your site
- Make sure all your images, video, and other forms of multimedia content are compressed.
- Build a Website with very high load time.
- Schedule Blog posts so that you stick to your routine of updating the content of your website.

The most crucial point is understanding the user intent behind searching a particular query.

11. Hiring SEO Experts

Hiring the right SEO expert could finish your search or finish your business. When searched in any region there are always significant amount of SEO agencies in every area.

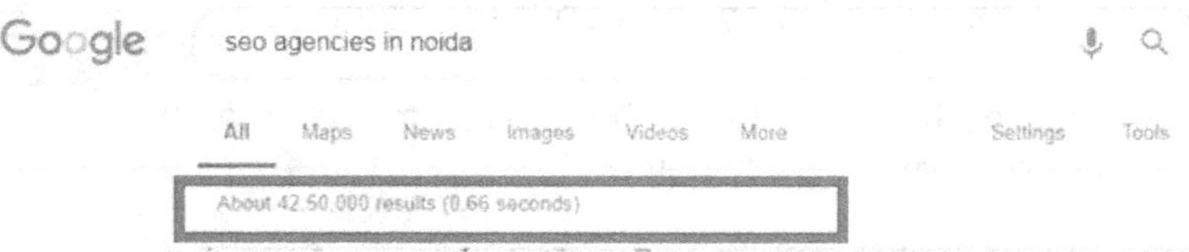

The one reason behind rapid boost of these SEO agencies is the dialogue " Sir as you know websites don't get ranked overnight, so it will take time for me to rank it" and by the time it ranks or doesn't, you have 6 monthly payment instalments already done, and you switch to a new expert and this cycle continues and your business is shut.

Well either you can hire an individual SEO consultant generally, freelancers or SEO agencies which work with companies of a decent size. No matter what, be equipped with tools that will save you time and money. These tools are the questions that you should ask before handing down your project and some sample answers you may expect.

Here we go-

1. How can you improve SEO rankings?

Without a severe SEO strategy, you do not have any significant results.

You may see small sporadic outcomes, but you will never see consistent increases in traffic if you choose to target keywords at random or build links.

What this means is that all good SEO, independent or agency workers have a process.

You may not be able to say: "We will get X, Y, and Z links," but what they can say is as follows: "We start with an on-site SEO technical audit to determine any area for rapid gains. Then we can determine the best keywords.
The automated, low-quality backlinks are commonly used for the building of spam links.

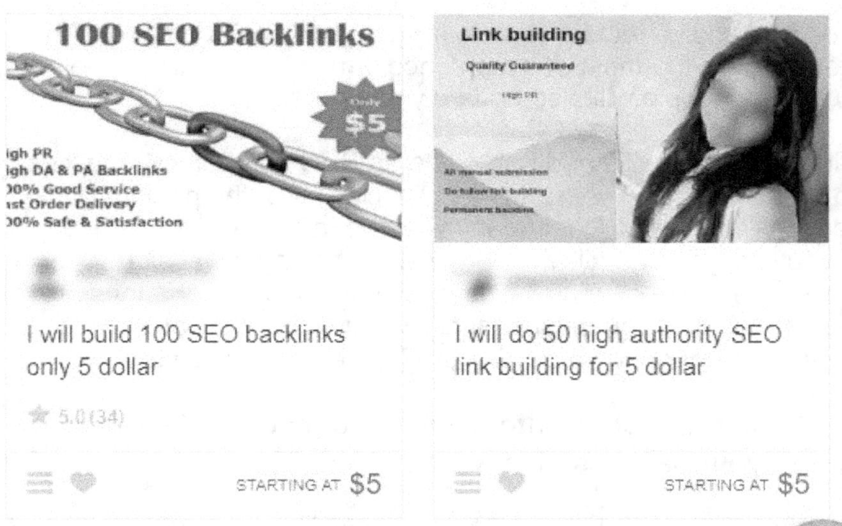

Think of the typical Fiverr.com gigs, where hundreds or thousands of useful links can be purchased for 5 to 10 dollars. A single useful link will cost at least 20 dollars, which is a good scenario.
If someone promises many links to you and works out at $1 or less per link, go the opposite way.

2. How can SEO be done with low budget?

Good content, links and strategy will cost your business. It can be done on a budget but not everything. People who sell a hundred blog posts and thousands of backlinks do not last long, neither the seller, not the buyer.

Though these configurations may appear as perfect budget SEO options, they usually cost your business more than one way as when sites are penalized. It takes even more effort to remove these shady links. Poor writing of content, faculty development code, and shady backlinks can damage your business. Give such examples to make the customer know that he has these options as well.

3. How will you explain to me the changes you have made to my website?

You will receive regular reports from a good SEO company. The frequency is the most common once a month (typically at the end), but some people will also update you weekly.

First of all, you will need to provide an SEO company with access to (at least part of) your website. This is one of the principal reasons why an SEO company you can trust needs to be hired. If you like, you can alleviate any risk by having a website developer make changes. The visible result is that changes are slower and that you must ensure that the communication between your developer and your SEO firm is open and consistent.

4. Can you share information and results on some of your past customers?

Shopping for an SEO company is exactly like shopping. You want to see reviews, reports, case studies of their past clients. You should not expect the SEO Company to hand out their whole book of past clients, but be happy if you get 2-3 customers which showed significant results.

If the company can't give an example of legitimate customers, then that is a massive warning that they don't have SEO skills of that level.

Next, you should ask about their longest active customer: Most significant problems with shady SEO companies is that they are using risky short-term tactics. They want to show customers fast results, not caring if they do anything that will put the site at risk in the future.If you interviewed a long time ago, SEO company and their longest active customer has been with them for less than a year; this is a red flag.

5.   Do you always work according to Google practices?

Google's best practices (and to a lesser extent, Bing's and Yahoo's) are critical to sustainable traffic growth.

Google applies approximately 500 updates per year. The purpose of all these updates is one: to provide searchers with better results. In essence, the guidelines are the "golden rules" published by every search engine.

Google isn't happy if you violate the rules. That is why some algorithms that penalize a lot of manipulative sites have been published like Panda, Penguin and Hummingbird.

6.   Which tools are you going to work with?

The word "tool" usually describes a variety of SEO applications. You can process much information in a short time by using tools. That can save a ton of time and money that's good for all. However, there are several tools like
  - Reporting Tools like Google Analytics and SEO Metrics
  - Link Building Tools like Ahref
  - Technical SEO tools like SEO Frog
  - Research Tools like Buzzstream

Most of these tools are excellent. However, if you are aiming for pure link building practices, they are the worst for your website as they are of shallow quality and can lead to Penalties.
If your SEO Company mentions tools like Xrumer or Senuke, you can stay away.

7.   What happens if your contract is terminated?

This is indeed for your protection because these SEO experts sign up for some minimum period, generally 3-6months. And at some point of time if you are unable to afford the pricing or the search ranking of the website are going down.

Know in advance if there are any fees for termination and how will they give back the controls of the website.

8. Are you updated with the latest algorithm changes

There are more than 500 algorithm changes every year that have a minor impact on your website. However, your SEO Expert should be aware of the major ones like

- Google Hummingbird
- Google Panda
-Google Penguin-
Google Mobile-Friendly Update
-Google Payday Update

It is a good idea to talk on phone or Skype call regarding these algorithms as an email could have a researched reply.

9. What type of SEO will you perform?

At least once you hire a company, there should be a basic technical audit SEO. They probably aren't very good SEOs when this isn't part of their process.

Technical SEO includes all the background aspects of SEO, which are still important for search engines. The underlying technical SEO consists all in identifying and addressing errors in the web crawler, 404 pages, redirecting problems, and evaluating site navigation.

10. Can you ensure our website ranks first for an initial search term?

This is the easiest way to remove fake SEO services from legitimate SEO services.

If an SEO expert is guaranteeing rank one on Google, this solely means that quality SEO should be able to increase your search traffic over time consistently, but they cannot guarantee specific keyword rankings. If that's your most significant promise, go the other way because no SEO expert knows the exact Google algorithm, when will it change and Google penalties can come out of anywhere.

There is a significant warning; however: some SEO could ask you what keyword you target or suggest. You could offer a guarantee if you target a very easy keyword that has very less competition. Note that guaranteeing and securing top position in the search results are two different things. The guarantee usually means you expect to rank one for an easy term, but if you can't help it, you will receive some reimbursement.

11. What is the payment structure?

Various SEO enterprises use various payment structures.
You need to know how much you have to pay to help you make a difference in your budget and exactly when.

Because SEO can be carried out in many various ways, the project can be carried out by many consultants. So they might have a project price ranging from $1,000 up to $7,500.Another feasible option is to pay by the hour, which is popular amongst the freelancers.

Expect an invoice in 30, 60 or 90 days.

12. Why should we hire you and not the competition?

If you get a reply like "We are cheap," " We will get you faster results" and "You will get more backlinks." With these answers, proceed cautiously.

Good SEO does not come cheap. Ask how the cost is divided between different services.

13. How to contact you?

SEO is different from other services because more than a few times a month, you do not usually need to contact your SEO company.

However, you want to be able to catch up so soon as possible, if anything goes wrong or you have to discuss an important issue.

Find out what communication methods they choose and tell them yours (you ought to ask somewhere). Also, ask how to contact them in the event of an emergency (if the site has fallen or search traffic dropped dramatically).

Conclusion

Next time you hire SEO experts, shoot them with these questions. Being from the same industry, we know filtration of quality seo experts will be very fast based on these questions. However, your cost and their efforts will be saved.

12. Social Media and SEO

Do you know that an average person checks out his phone about 80 times a day and scrolls his news feed? Some companies are taking advantage of the fact and designing their posts and campaigns in such a way so that it sticks on their news feed and they engage.

If you carefully analyze the websites that rank top on Google, you will see that they have diversified social signals from different social mediums. You need to analyze what source is working for you and accordingly optimize for that source.

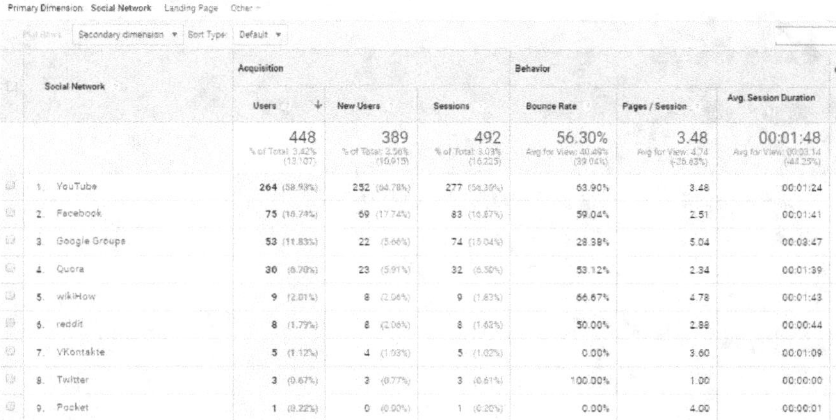

Primary Dimension: Social Network   Landing Page   Other

Secondary dimension ▼   Sort Type: Default ▼

Social Network	Acquisition			Behavior		
	Users ↓	New Users	Sessions	Bounce Rate	Pages / Session	Avg. Session Duration
	448 % of Total: 3.42% (13,107)	389 % of Total: 2.56% (10,915)	492 % of Total: 3.03% (16,225)	56.30% Avg for View: 40.49% (39.04%)	3.48 Avg for View: 4.74 (-26.63%)	00:01:48 Avg for View: 00:03:14 (-44.25%)
1. YouTube	264 (58.93%)	252 (64.78%)	277 (56.30%)	63.90%	3.48	00:01:24
2. Facebook	75 (16.74%)	69 (17.74%)	83 (16.87%)	59.04%	2.51	00:01:41
3. Google Groups	53 (11.83%)	22 (5.66%)	74 (15.04%)	28.38%	5.04	00:03:47
4. Quora	30 (6.70%)	23 (5.91%)	32 (6.50%)	53.12%	2.34	00:01:39
5. wikiHow	9 (2.01%)	8 (2.06%)	9 (1.83%)	66.67%	4.78	00:01:43
6. reddit	8 (1.79%)	8 (2.06%)	8 (1.62%)	50.00%	2.88	00:00:44
7. VKontakte	5 (1.12%)	4 (1.03%)	5 (1.02%)	0.00%	3.60	00:01:09
8. Twitter	3 (0.67%)	3 (0.77%)	3 (0.61%)	100.00%	1.00	00:00:00
9. Pocket	1 (0.22%)	0 (0.00%)	1 (0.20%)	0.00%	4.00	00:00:01

The above screenshot depicts user behavior of people from different social mediums.

What Google had to say about Social Signals?

In 2010, Google webmasters released a video on Youtube featuring Matt Cutt. According to him, social signals are considered to be an essential factor in the ranking of the website on the search engines. He explained that it is currently being used in the real-time search index, and they are continually trying to figure out how they would be expanding it more into the different search areas.

(Contradiction) Why does Google ignore Social Signals?

Google doesn't rank your website by considering the likes as well as the number of shares you have received on your social media post. Anyone can crack the system and get a countless number of likes as well as shares. That wouldn't be a fair game. People would cheat more and more to gain a higher ranking. Plus, people share on social media platforms every second. So it's not possible for Google to catch up with the posts. That would make it too difficult for search engines to rank the websites.

There are sites like www.like4like.org, www.addmefast.me and www.followlike.net where you can exchange likes, shares, follows and even blog post. So it means that your content might have been shared 1000 times but not a single person read it. So this is the reason some social signals are ignored.

12.1 Optimizing Social Media

Social media optimizing refers to ways of optimizing social media platforms in order to increase brand awareness about a product to increase its sales.

 Here's how you can do it:

Optimize the Social Media Profile

People take purchase decisions in less than 3 seconds when they look at the social profiles of a company. Following are major points to take care: -

- The bio should give them a clear picture of what your business is all about.
-Cover picture and profile picture should represent your brand colours.
-The website should be the first call to action.
- A visitor should know ways to purchase your service or contact you.
It's crucial that all of your social media accounts need to consist of the same image as it would lead to an increase in brand recognition.

Post Updates Regularly

Creating an attractive social media profile isn't enough. You need to post updates regularly. You need to provide your customers with regular updates about your products and services.

Research about the audience demographic on social media pages. See who your audience is, what their age group is, and when they are active during the week and the day, what languages they are speaking, which city they belong to and so on. Accordingly, schedule posts with applications like "Hootsuite."

Build Partnerships

Research for influencers who would be interested in partnering up with you. This would give you potential customers for your product. Your brand awareness will increase and overall, you will find more audience for your social networks.

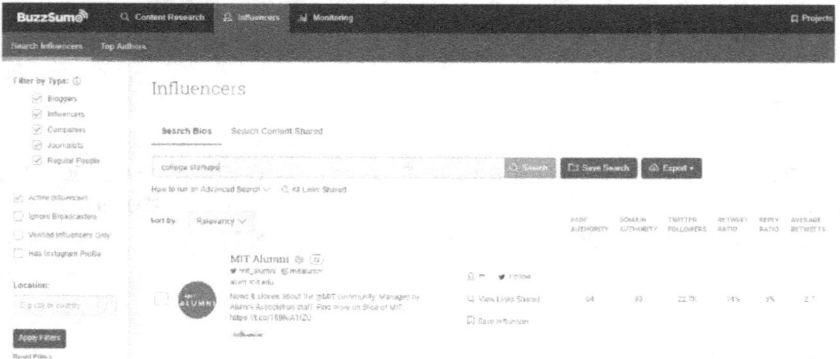

Use "Search Influencer" feature of a tool named Buzzsumo to get a list of influencers who talk about your topic. Remember the conversion ratio when you contact them for partnerships is around 4% to 5%. When you send an email to 100 Influencers, then five might consider for some form of strategic alliances.

Improve Social Updates

In case you would love to watch the sight of your social media posts to be spreading like wildfire, you need to optimize them correctly. You need to follow these points briefly:

- Perfect headlines for the post.
-Catchy images that force people to stop while they are scrolling the news feed.
- Use hashtags so that people searching for your content can quickly find it.

- Schedule at a time when the maximum of your audience is active.
-Encourage them to follow you across networks via having something unique for each network like for Instagram you can share a quote on stories, Facebook: live videos for interaction with the audience; Twitter can have AMA (Ask Me Anything) sessions. The point is to have something unique for each social networks.
-Stay up to date with hourly trends and be the first person to respond.

You Need To Engage

Engage as much as you can with the audience that has liked or followed you across networks. Tell them that they can contact you anytime and try to respond to as many comments, questions or feedback as you can. This is the best way to increase brand loyalty amongst the people who have followed you.

Hashtags increase Searchability

Every social media groups posts according to hashtags, this is how we see trends happening on Twitter. It might be hard to use the perfect hashtag to define your post. Use a maximum of 5-7 hashtags to define your post.

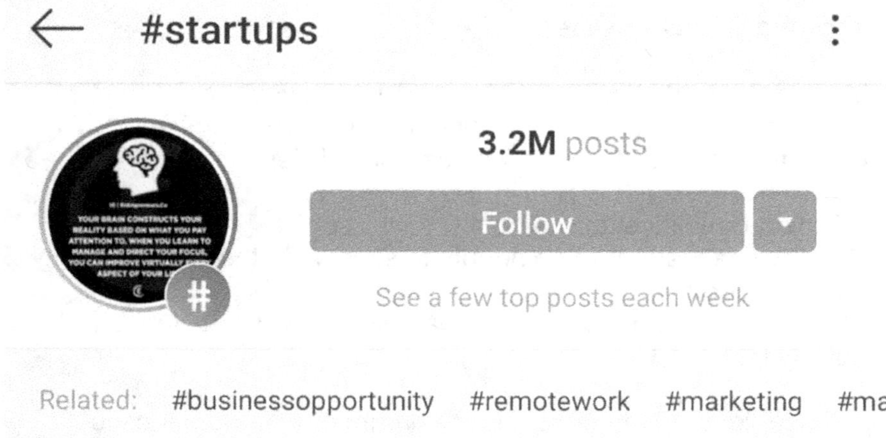

Social networks like Instagram and Twitter, give users the option to follow hashtags that are relevant to them.

Conclusion

Social media is all about scheduling the right content for the right audience at the most appropriate time and the most important is to do it regularly. If you are starting out and you think your content is of very high quality, consider paid advertising on social mediums so that people get to know about your content.

13. SEO Myths

Even SEO has myths that are unknowingly spread by bloggers, authenticated by experts, and followed by the whole community. Some of them induce fear in the minds of people, whereas others put them into a relaxed mode. Let us look at them one by one.

1.   Myth: Google will penalize slow websites.

Reality: As per Google, "It will only affect pages that deliver the slowest experience to users and will only affect a small percentage of queries. The intent of the search query is still a sound signal, so a slow webpage may still rank highly if it has great, relevant content." Page Speed contributes to ranking but is not the sole factor.

2.   Myth: News Releases will boost your ranking.

Reality: Google automatically ignores these links as they are from the company themselves and are not natural links. Google also said that these type of link should be nofollowed (Links with rel="nofollow" tell the search engine to ignore the links and not pass page rank, and they do not impact search engine rankings). News releases were an old tradition; do not spend money on them now.

3.   Myth: Meta Tags are not relevant anymore.

Reality: Matt Cutts said that Google doesn't use the keywords and description metatag in page ranking, but they are still relevant, and you should spend time on them. People click a particular website seeing what Meta Tag has to say about the Content.

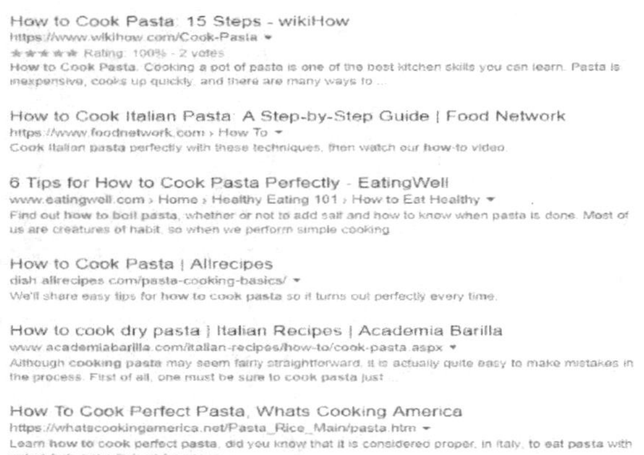

For the search "How to Cook Pasta" meta description too has some say in understanding what the user intent it.

4. Myth: Google doesn't care about security certificates.

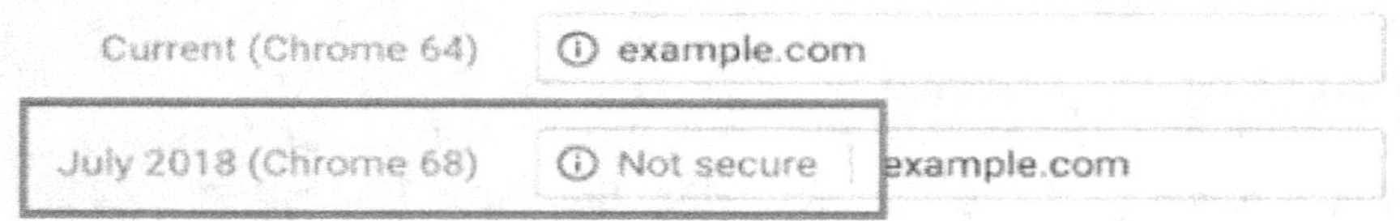

Reality: Google confirmed since 2014 that HTTPS/SSL is a ranking factor and increases website credibility. Data from Google Chrome shows that more than 70% of the users visit Secure sites, and since July 2018, Google has marked and reminds visitors that the websites are" Not Secure." So it is high time you get an HTTPs certificate for your website. You can get free HTTPs or SSL certificate from *www.sslforfree.com* or *www.letsencrypt.org*.

5. Myth: More Content = Higher rank on the web.

Reality: It all depends on the Content quality, not on the quantity. Try answering the visitor's intent via blog posts. Regularity in updation indeed shows that your website is fresh, but this is not a factor for ranking. It depends upon the level of your content.

6. Myth: SEO for once and relax for life.

Reality: Google, on an average, has 500 small updates every year. Ranking signals change over time. They vary from query to query, from day to day and from user to user. There's a lot of personalization required.

7. Myth: Automated SEO is blackhat or spammy.

Reality: Well, there is nothing wrong with using automation to manage all your channels. In today's era, companies that do automation are the ones that have time to plan more diversification to engage users. Imagine you are scheduling your posts, liking posts that have a specific hashtag, engaging with the Instagram community on automation basis. Everything, when done according to the guidelines of the Social Network & the search engine, encourages users to interact with the Brand.

8. Myth: Using a service that promises to register your site with "hundreds of search engines" is suitable for your site's rankings.

Reality: Have you seen that email where Nigerian prince who desperately needs your help to get a large amount of money smuggled out of his country for which you will be rewarded? '

Avoid all the services that promise overnight ranking of your content. They are spam, and this will lead to your downgrade in your rankings.

9. Myth: Spending lots of money in paid search help your organic rankings.

Reality: No, a paid search does not help in organic rankings. This is a simple formula that every company that is looking forward to investing in paid campaigns should remember. Paid search and rankings are entirely disconnected from each other.

10. Myth: First, you get your site launched, then start with SEO efforts.

Reality: Imagine building a home first and then doing the electrical wiring throughout the house. Though it is possible, but for that, you need to tear out the walls to get the installation done. That is how SEO needs to be done. When you are writing content for the website or drawing a wireframe for every page, keywords optimization and planning should be your first step.

11. Myth: Our SEO firm is endorsed/approved by Google.

Reality: There are so many companies that have this logo on their website that they are Google approved partners, and that is how they take projects. There is nothing known as Google approved partners, if you run an AdWords campaign via Google or any search engine for say then you can call yourself as their partner. This is a hack to increase sales.

12. Myth: There's no such thing as mobile SEO.

Reality: Google can now detect usability issues that the user faces while mobile browsing. If the website is not optimized for mobile browsing experience, then you might see a drop of your ranking on a search engine for users searching on Mobile.

13. Myth: Great content equals (i.e., automatically leads to) high rankings.

Reality: While I was writing this chapter election are going on in India. So, I had this question, does outstanding policy means a successful politician? No, right. You have a substantial content that deserves to be ranked but does not, as no one knows about it or your site architecture is misleading to the spiders.

Do not be solely dependent on the content; do marketing on various social networks, build links on multiple blogs, answer people on Quora. In short, let people know you exist.

14. Myth: It's important for your rankings that you update your home page frequently.

Reality: Plenty of Static Websites are doing just fine. Freshness may be helpful but not required to maintain a high ranking. If you have strong domain authority, you can maintain a top position on a search engine for a very long time.

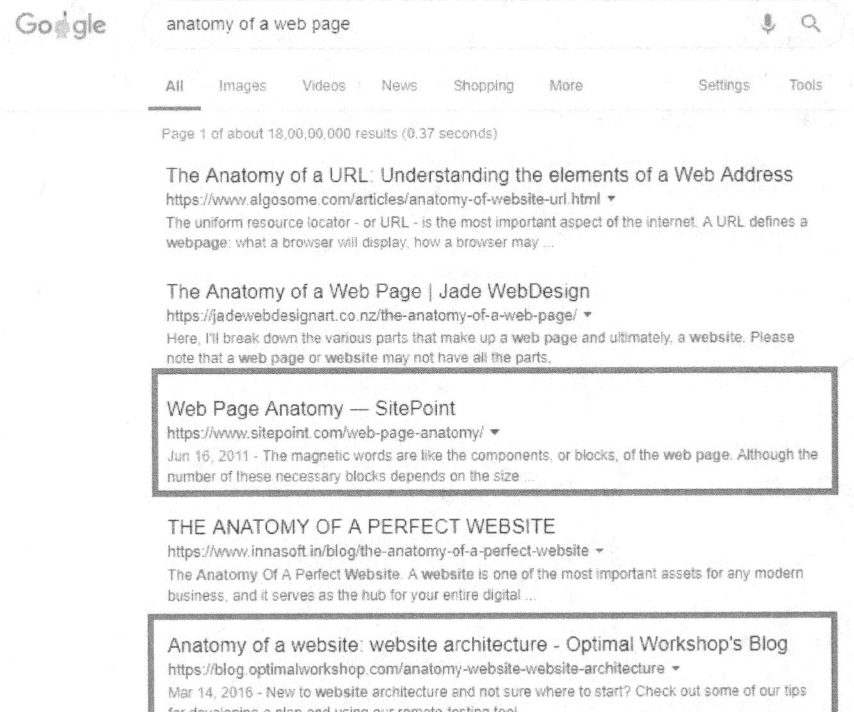

When you search "Anatomy of a Webpage" on Google, there are sites that are ranking from 2011 or 2016, so domain authority does come into play.

15. Myth: I've got lots of links, so I don't need to build more.

Reality: Search Engine look at various factors when it comes to link building. Old links indicate authority in your content, whereas new links show freshness and relevance. So it is a good idea to have both.

Conclusion

These Myths change over time, and plenty of new ones come as Search Engine update their algorithm. The only thing that you should remember is to follow the basics of SEO while developing or marketing your website.

Please Help

What Did You Think of SEO for Startups?

First of all, thank you for purchasing this book **SEO for Startups.** I know you could have picked any number of books to read, but you picked this book and for that I am extremely grateful.

I have made this book the mission of my life and **plan to update it every two months** so that this it never gets outdated.

If you enjoyed this book and found some benefit in reading this, I'd like to hear from you and hope that you could take some time to post a **review on Amazon.** I personally read each and every review which is the biggest motivation factor for me to work even harder.

 Your feedback and support will help me to greatly improve the writing craft for future projects and make this book even better.

I wish you all the best in your future success!